This book belongs to:
Ma
P9-DMO-154

Barnes & Noble Shakespeare

David Scott Kastan
Series Editor

BARNES & NOBLE SHAKESPEARE features newly edited texts of the plays prepared by the world's premiere Shakespeare scholars. Each edition provides new scholarship with an introduction, commentary, unusually full and informative notes, an account of the play as it would have been performed in Shakespeare's theaters, and an essay on how to read Shakespeare's language.

DAVID SCOTT KASTAN is the Old Dominion Foundation Professor in the Humanities at Columbia University and one of the world's leading authorities on Shakespeare.

Barnes & Noble Shakespeare
Published by Barnes & Noble
122 Fifth Avenue
New York, NY 10011
www.barnesandnoble.com/shakespeare

© 2007 Barnes & Noble, Inc.

All rights reserved. No part of this publication may be reproduced, stored in a retrieval system, or transmitted, in any form or by any means, electronic, mechanical, photocopying, recording, or otherwise, without prior written permission from the publisher.

Image on p. 294:
William Shakespeare, *Comedies, Histories, & Tragedies*, London, 1623, Bequest of Stephen Whitney Phoenix, Rare Book & Manuscript Library, Columbia University.

Barnes & Noble Shakespeare and the Barnes & Noble Shakespeare colophon are trademarks of Barnes & Noble, Inc.

ISBN-13: 978-1-4114-0037-5

        Library of Congress Cataloging-in-Publication Data

Shakespeare, William, 1564–1616.
  Macbeth / [William Shakespeare].
    p. cm. — (Barnes & Noble Shakespeare)
  Includes bibliographical references.
  ISBN-13: 978-1-4114-0037-5 (alk. paper)

  1. Macbeth, King of Scotland, 11th cent.—Drama. 2. Scotland—Kings and rulers—Drama. 3. Regicides—Drama. I. Title. II. Series: Shakespeare, William, 1564–1616. Works. 2006.

PR2823.A1 2006
822.3'3–dc22   2006009005

Printed and bound in the United States.
20

MACBETH

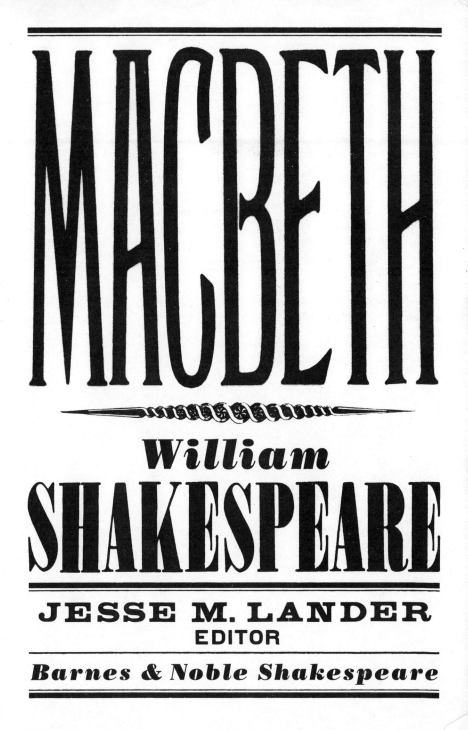

William
SHAKESPEARE

JESSE M. LANDER
EDITOR

Barnes & Noble Shakespeare

Contents

Introduction to *Macbeth*
by Jesse M. Lander

*acbeth* is the only Shakespearean tragedy that has a villain as its hero. Shakespeare's other tragic heroes are morally compromised in various ways, but none actively and knowingly embrace evil. Macbeth willingly pursues a murder that he knows will result in his "deep damnation" (1.7.20), creating an interpretive problem. Is Macbeth merely a vigorous criminal who gets his inevitable and just punishment at the play's end? Certainly Malcolm, who calls Macbeth a "butcher" (5.8.69) and Angus, who refers to him as a "dwarfish thief" (5.2.22), encourage such a view. The difficulty with these assessments is that they do not accord with audiences' experience of Macbeth. Whatever his faults—and they are multitudinous—Macbeth engages the audience, and despite his acts of dire cruelty, he never entirely loses his appeal. Indeed, it is hard to see how the play could succeed as a tragedy if the audience simply adopted Malcolm's point of view. It would turn the play into a moral homily. Consequently, a long critical tradition has lionized Macbeth by emphasizing his energetic, daring, and poetic imagination. Regarded in this way, Macbeth is seen not as a diminished and increasingly desperate reprobate, but as a character who exhibits grandeur and is, in fact, sublime. Macbeth becomes part of a tragic pantheon that includes the mythological figures of Prometheus

and Icarus alongside Christopher Marlowe's Faustus and Milton's Satan, all of them doomed losers who rebel against an order that appears to them unjust. While such a view perhaps makes better sense of the experience of the play than does stern moralizing on the sinfulness of ambition, it also transforms the complex problem of human evil into an exploration of the heroic individual's struggle against a hostile or indifferent universe: acts of imagination and acts of rebellion are identified, and the true source of evil is located in the blank fatality of a world that constrains the freedom of the individual. However, this view of Macbeth also fails fully to accord with audiences' experience. If Macbeth is not merely a criminal, neither is he an unproblematic hero. In order to get at the heart of the play, the central paradox of the heroic criminal or criminal hero must be explored, not resolved in favor of one term or the other. This means thinking seriously about the problem of evil; and though there is a broad consensus about the centrality of evil in Macbeth, there is, unsurprisingly, very little agreement about what precisely constitutes that evil. One way around this difficulty is to ask not how we ought to define evil, but to ask instead how the play's particular engagement with evil was shaped by the peculiar pressures and concerns of its day. Such contextual knowledge will not explain the mystery of iniquity, but it may help account for the play's famous ambiguity, an ambiguity centrally embodied in its hero-villain.

Macbeth depicts, from the start, a world in which treachery and ambition have dissolved the social fabric. Ambition, an aggressive self-assertion that threatens the customary social order, is the motive for treachery, the willful abrogation of loyalty and the refusal of social bonds. When Macbeth meditates on the murder of Duncan, he reminds himself that his king is "here in double trust" (1.7.12), and then enumerates not two but three bonds of obligation: Duncan is his kinsman, his sovereign, and his guest, and as each requires Macbeth's loyalty and protection. Macbeth acknowledges the force of these layered social obligations at the very moment in which he prepares to violate them in pursuit of the crown. The notion that Macbeth's tragic flaw is ambition is a tired cliché that explains very little, and yet it would be a mistake to dismiss ambition as a motive altogether. Lady Macbeth, who knows her husband, says that he is "not without ambition, but without / The illness that should attend it" (1.5.18–19). Macbeth himself says that he has "no spur / To prick the sides of my intent, but only / Vaulting ambition" (1.7.25–27) even as Lady Macbeth enters to provide what he lacks. Ross condemns "thriftless ambition" as an excessive appetite that leads to its own demise. Ambition and treachery work as powerful solvents loosening the bonds of social order, but though they may find their fiercest and most emphatic expression in the Macbeths, they permeate the entire world of the play.

The play opens on a "hurly-burly" world, a violent and tumultuous place in which loyalty already seems precarious. First the witches appear, accompanied by thunder and lightning, to announce that they will meet again after "the battle's lost and won" (1.1.4); next King Duncan and his party meet a bloody Captain, who graphically describes how "brave Macbeth" (1.2.16) has "unseamed" (1.2.22) and beheaded the rebellious Macdonwald. The battle also includes the defeat of Norwegian forces allied with the rebels and the capture of "that most disloyal traitor, / The Thane of Cawdor" (1.2.52–53). Duncan's disappointment with the Thane of Cawdor, on whom he "built an absolute trust," forces him to concede that "There's no art / To find the mind's construction in the face" (1.4.11–12). Though Duncan's belated understanding and misplaced trust do not speak well for his political wisdom, this moment points to a significant problem not only in the world of *Macbeth* but in Shakespeare's tragedies more generally, and indeed in the wider world of early modern Europe.

The possibility that people were not what they appeared or claimed to be was given new urgency by the religious changes that transformed early modern Europe. The struggles between Catholics and Protestants in post-Reformation Europe led to a widespread sense that one's neighbors, friends, even family might entertain secret and alien religious affiliations or convictions. In a world unprepared to accept religious pluralism, the split in Western Christianity led to the persecution of religious minorities. The Protestant Reformation not only produced controversy and conflict, religious wars being the most extreme form, but also contributed to a new sense of religious identity as an interior experience—a dynamic that held true for the godly minority, who felt themselves to be the only "true" Protestants in a mass of unregenerate sinners, as well as for those Catholics who outwardly conformed to the liturgical demands of the English church while secretly maintaining allegiance to the Church of Rome. This situation produced a new emphasis on the distinction between inward disposition and outward conformity; Elizabeth I famously declared that she had no desire to make "windows into men's souls," but she did insist that her subjects worship according to a uniform liturgy. Those who refused to comply were labeled "recusants" and were subject to fines and, in some cases, imprisonment. The essayist Michel de Montaigne, who experienced the deadly turmoil of religious warfare in France, remarked that "the worst of these wars is that the cards are so shuffled that your enemy is distinguished from yourself by no apparent mark either of language or bearing, and has been brought up in the same law and customs and the same atmosphere, so that it is hard to avoid confusion and disorder." The unnerving possibility of home-bred enemies who are indistinguishable from the rest of the population could and did breed paranoia, but not all persecutions and conspiracies were imagined.

Paranoia and anxiety about the loyalty of English Catholics were given new momentum in November 1605, when a small group of militant Catholics, disappointed in their hopes for a Catholic succession in 1603 and increasingly convinced that the new King would not reverse the strict penal statutes on Catholics, attempted to blow up the King at the opening of Parliament. While many of the details of the Gunpowder Plot remain obscure, there is little doubt that the vast majority of English subjects believed that there had been a Jesuit-inspired plot to destroy the King and Parliament—a plot that was providentially exposed through the wisdom of King James himself. The Gunpowder Plot, sensational evidence of a Catholic fifth column committed to the destruction of Protestant England, reverberates throughout _Macbeth_. Its echoes can be heard not only in the play's focus on political assassination but also in its fascination with _equivocation_—a term that became notorious in the wake of the plot. Father Garnet, one of the Jesuits implicated in the conspiracy, defended the practice of mental reservation or equivocation that sanctioned giving misleading answers when being interrogated by a hostile authority. The most explicit reference to the Gunpowder Plot appears in the Porter's remark: "here's an equivocator that could swear in both the scales against either scale, who committed treason enough for God's sake, yet could not equivocate to Heaven" (2.3.8–11). Beyond this specific example, the theme of ambiguous and equivocal speech is suffused throughout the play.

The witches speak strange paradoxes—"When the battle's lost and won" (1.1.4); "Fair is foul, and foul is fair"(1.1.11)—that defy resolution. Macbeth, of course, only discovers this at the play's end when, facing defeat, he comes to "doubt th' equivocation of the fiend / That lies like truth." (5.5.43–44). The linguistic disorder of the "juggling fiends" who "palter with us in a double sense" (5.8.19–20) is not limited to the witches. One of the play's most puzzling scenes occurs when Macduff, having fled from Scotland, offers his services to Malcolm only to be met with suspicion and duplicity. In order to test Macduff, Malcolm falsely confesses to sins that outstrip even the tyranny of Macbeth. When Macduff finally loses patience and condemns Malcolm as "accursed" (4.3.107), Malcolm praises Macduff's integrity and confesses that his subterfuge was merely a test to determine whether Macduff had been sent by Macbeth. Clearly what Malcolm claims as "My first false speaking" (4.3.130) is not "the equivocation of the fiend" but the sort of deceptive language that occurs under tyranny when none dare speak frankly. Another form of linguistic corruption, the slippery language of insinuation, appears in the short exchange between Macbeth and Banquo that takes place immediately before Duncan's murder, where Macbeth offers unspecified "honor" (2.1.26) in exchange for Banquo's complicity, but the deformation of language under tyranny is most evident in the veiled conversation between Lennox and an unnamed lord in Act Three, scene six. Lennox's account of recent affairs is a masterpiece of ironic understatement: "The gracious Duncan / Was pitied of Macbeth; marry, he was dead" (3.6.3–4). Macbeth comes to recognize his own role in this process when he anticipates receiving the empty "mouth-honor" (5.3.27) of his alienated subjects, who secretly hate him. The play's emphasis on the shiftiness of language is, of course, not only a response to the Gunpowder Plot; it points to a more general social condition in which language, rather than serving as a social cement, becomes instead a vehicle for hypocrisy and subterfuge. This situation was surely exacerbated by the perception of a new social mobility, especially in London, a city that had seen enormous population growth largely as a consequence of immigration. The city held forth the promise of advancement for the industrious, but the underside of this fantasy was a substantial anxiety about upstarts and imposters. These social conditions, along with the fact of religious division, created a deep unease about the legibility as well as the legitimacy of the social world.

In England, where the official religion was repeatedly and drastically altered during the course of the sixteenth century, access to the sacred became a deeply divisive issue. The Reformation's promotion of the priesthood of all believers raised enduring questions about the authority of the ecclesiastical institutions that claimed to administer the sacred. In addition, debates about the clergy, the sacraments, and practices like pilgrimage and the veneration of saints cast doubt on traditional practices that had offered a coherent vision of the universe and the relationship between the supernatural and natural worlds. *Macbeth*, like *Hamlet*, reveals an almost obsessive concern with what Macbeth calls "supernatural soliciting" (1.3.131). Both plays offer oblique commentary on the difficulties of interpreting the supernatural in order to warrant human action, a commentary that is directly relevant to the struggles over ecclesiastical authority that were roiling Europe.

Macbeth's spectacular opening—thunder and lightning and witches on a heath—would have immediately prepared the audience for supernatural events. Today, audience members may doubt the predictive power of meteorology, but we accept that there is a scientific basis for the weather; early modern people, in contrast, tended to view storms as diabolical disruptions, signs of disorder in the heavens often attributed to demonic agency and frequently associated with witchcraft. Though England never had witch hunts of the sort seen in Continental Europe, there was a legal framework for the punishment of witchcraft, and witches were an accepted reality. The last execution for witchcraft in England was in 1685, but the laws against witchcraft were not repealed until 1736. Though witchcraft belief was central to the thought and culture of both the intellectual elite and the common people, it did not meet with universal assent. There were occasional expressions of skepticism, like Reginald Scot's *The Discoverie of Witchcraft* (1584), but these were met with stinging rebuttals that accused doubters of heterodoxy and even atheism. Indeed, James I had been personally involved in the prosecution of witches when in Scotland and had written a book, *Daemonologie* (1603), defending the reality of witchcraft. Yet the play's engagement with the supernatural is something much more than a nod toward the intellectual interests of the reigning monarch and patron of Shakespeare's acting company.

Even before the arrival of James I, the problem of witchcraft was being taken seriously in England. Historians of witchcraft have frequently sought long-term social explanations for the witchcraft persecutions that swept early modern Europe. The fact that the vast majority of those accused were women, usually old and frequently marginalized, has encouraged the notion that witch hunts were fundamentally driven by an unconscious fear of women and their sexuality. Witch hunting thus served to manage the hostilities of a gynophobic culture, focusing aggression on the figure of the witch, who served as convenient scapegoat. *Macbeth* offers some support for this explanation; it is surely not accidental that a play haunted by witches is dominated in its early scenes

by Lady Macbeth, a female character who invokes demonic aid and renounces her gender: "Come, you spirits / That tend on mortal thoughts,
unsex me here / And fill me from the crown to the toe top-full / Of
direst cruelty" (1.5.39–42). The witches also provoke confusion over
gender. Banquo says, "You should be women, / And yet your beards forbid
me to interpret / That you are so" (1.3.45–47). They exhibit a sexual vora-
ciousness that was a regular feature in discussions of witches. The First
Witch, in particular, announces her insatiable desire—"I'll do, I'll do, and
I'll do" (1.3.10)—and plans to sexually exhaust a sailor ("I'll drain him dry
as hay"). James I in the preface to *Daemonologie* alludes to the power witches
have "of weakening the nature of some men, to make them unable for
women." Charges of impotence induced by enchantment were a regular
feature in witchcraft allegations, and Macbeth's bitter complaint about
his "barren scepter" blames the weird sisters for having placed a "fruitless
crown" (3.1.61–62) on his head.

The witch served as a lightning rod for a whole host of social
anxieties about gender, aging, and charity. At the same time, the witch
as a mediator who traffics in the supernatural played an important part
in intellectual debates of the period. For defenders of the belief in witchcraft, such figures were profound and necessary evidence of a spiritual
realm. The existence of demons was widely recognized as evidence of the
existence of God, and witches were useful precisely because they could
provide testimony concerning the existence of demons. Richard Baxter,
a seventeenth-century theologian, observes that witches and apparitions
are "sensible proof of spirits and another life, an argument of more direct
force than any speculations, or abstract reasonings." The common Protestant notion that, as King James writes, "all miracles, visions, prophecies,
and appearances of angels and good spirits are ceased," still allowed for
the appearance of diabolical spirits, producing a world only partially
disenchanted, in which demonic activity paradoxically served to support
faith in an omnipotent God.

Though they remain mysterious—we do not know whether they are human or supernatural, and their powers are indeterminate—there is no question that the weird sisters are not delusions but actually exist within the world of the play. Moreover, they are not the only supernatural element in the play. Most obviously there is the ghost of Banquo, an apparition that appears to only Macbeth and the audience. In addition, there is "A dagger of the mind" (2.1.38), a visual hallucination, and the voice that cries "Sleep no more!" (2.2.38), an aural hallucination. While the modern interest in psychology tends to read this series of uncanny examples in such a way that makes the sisters, if not outright hallucinations, then at least symbolic manifestations of Macbeth's own "black and deep desires" (1.4.51), there is a strong argument for seeing the psychological as a manifestation of the supernatural and not the other way around. The dagger and the voice may indeed proceed from Macbeth's "brainsickly" (2.2.49) mind, but it was widely believed that the devil could interfere with human perception, and when Lady Macbeth offers a similarly naturalistic explanation for the ghost ("This is the very painting of your fear" [3.4.61]), the audience can see that she is wrong. The hallucinations that Macbeth experiences before and after the murder may directly reflect his own agitation, which is real enough, but they may also be the result of demonic suggestion. They remain questionable, and that is, in part, the point.

Like *Hamlet*, *Macbeth* suggests that there is more in heaven and earth then is dreamt of in our philosophy. As in *Hamlet*, the existence of the supernatural is not in doubt; what remains a persistent problem is its proper interpretation. In what ways can the supernatural serve as a warrant for human action? Though both plays focus on strange eruptions of the supernatural—the apparition in *Hamlet* is either "a spirit of health or goblin damn'd" (*Hamlet*, 1.4.40)—they also provide an oblique commentary on traditional religious institutions that claimed to operate on the basis of supernatural authority, with consequences that were often no less horrible than the bloody slaughters staged in *Hamlet* and *Macbeth*. Nonetheless, while the two plays share an interest in the supernatural, there are also revealing differences. _Hamlet_ does not offer the world of nature as a robust alternative. Indeed, the corruption of the world is so extreme and so complete that nature itself is seen as part of the problem—generation, a key concern in _Macbeth_ and a positive value, can only lead in _Hamlet_ to more sin. For Hamlet, Denmark is "an unweeded garden / That grows to seed" (1.2.135–136); rejecting Ophelia and with her the possibility of procreation, he asks, "wouldst thou be a breeder of sinners?" (3.1.121–122) Hamlet's _contemptus mundi_ is joined, in the end, by an awareness of the "divinity that shapes our ends" (5.2.10); in contrast, Macbeth is unable to relinquish the notion that nature provides a powerful image of the good, and yet he also insists that life is "a tale / Told by an idiot, full of sound and fury, / Signifying nothing" (5.5.27–29).

Though Macbeth rejects the possibility of finding meaning in life, the play suggests not so much the supernatural consolation offered in _Hamlet_ but a faith in the ordinary rhythms of nature. Macbeth describes Duncan's wounds as "a breach in nature" (2.3.111), and in many ways this phrase could stand as a description of the play's action, which, like the sleepwalking of Lady Macbeth, is "a great perturbation in nature" (5.1.8). As the Old Man remarks of the darkness of the day, "'Tis unnatural, / Even like the deed that's done" (2.4.10–11). The Doctor observes: "Unnatural deeds / Do breed unnatural troubles" (5.1.64–65). Explicit references to the natural and the unnatural are reinforced by a network of organic images that insistently suggest that somewhere there is still an appropriate rhythm to life, a sequence of birth, growth, maturation, decay, and death. Duncan welcomes the victorious Macbeth using the language of cultivation: "I have begun to plant thee and will labor / To make thee full of growing" (1.4.28–29), and at the play's conclusion Malcolm promises to perform that "Which would be planted newly with the time" (5.8.65). As the assault on Macbeth begins, Malcolm proclaims, "Macbeth / Is ripe for shaking" (4.3.238–239), and Lennox describes their mission as "To dew the sovereign flower and drown the weeds" (5.2.30). But the single most powerful articulation of this vision of human life as part of a great and regular nature comes from Macbeth himself:

> I have lived long enough. My way of life
> Is fall'n into the sere, the yellow leaf,
> And that which should accompany old age,
> As honor, love, obedience, troops of friends,
> I must not look to have, but in their stead
> Curses, not loud but deep, mouth-honor, breath
> Which the poor heart would fain deny and dare not. (5.3.22–28)

There is something terrible and terribly sad about this elegiac reflection on the life that Macbeth might have had. The cadences have changed— instead of the restless energy that so frequently propels his verse, Macbeth here offers a steady and stately succession of monosyllables and near monosyllables. It's dreadfully simple and direct: like a curled autumnal leaf, Macbeth faces imminent extinction and will enjoy none of the things that should come with advanced age. The vision of social integration and gradual maturation foregone expresses a deep regard for a traditional social order in which the old are accorded love, respect, and honor, where the fruit of a long life includes "troops of friends." The image of "the sere, the yellow leaf" insists that human life, part of the wider world of nature, exhibits a regular rhythm of growth, flourishing, and decay. Macbeth knows that his actions have destroyed what should have been, and this painful knowledge makes him something more than the "butcher" excoriated by Malcolm.

In addition to invoking the positive value of the natural order assaulted by both the weird sisters and the Macbeths, the play also offers a fleeting glimpse of a benevolent supernatural order. Act Four, scene three, the only scene set in England, presents a sustained consideration of the English King's healing powers. The "most pious Edward" (3.6.27) referred to in the play is Edward the Confessor, an eleventh-century king who was subsequently sainted and was held to have been the first English king to touch for the king's evil (scrofula). This "most miraculous work in this good King" (4.3.147) is the play's only direct evidence of a benign supernatural order. Along with his healing touch, Edward has "a heavenly gift of prophecy" (4.3.157), a detail that contrasts directly with the malignant oracles of the weird sisters, imperfect speakers who palter in a double sense. These gifts and "sundry blessings hang about his throne / That speak him full of grace" (4.3.158–159). This moment provides a sharp and immediate contrast with the following scene in which the Scottish Doctor admits that Lady Macbeth's case exceeds his art: "More needs she the divine than the physician" (5.1.67). This pointed juxtaposition suggests that Scotland is a godforsaken place, prone to violence and infected by demonic powers; England, in contrast, is a peaceful realm ruled by a graceful monarch.

The contrast established between England and Scotland could not have been entirely pleasing to Shakespeare's royal patron, King James, who, of course, was a Scot and indeed still King of Scotland. *Macbeth* perpetuates the usual English stereotype of their neighbors to the north: Scotland is a bloody and violent place populated by a rude and barbarous people. What the Scots lack in refinement they make up for in martial vigor and undiluted masculinity. In contrast, the English, derided as effeminate and weak by Macbeth, are depicted as an orderly nation led by a sacred king. Indeed, though many have seen in *Macbeth* a calculated attempt to flatter the new Scottish King of England, the play's vision of a violent and witch infested Scotland hardly seems celebratory. However, the argument for royal flattery is not based solely on the play's treatment of Scotland and witchcraft, but also on its presentation of sacred kingship itself.

James I had well-established views on the exalted status and expansive powers of the monarch that he shared in speeches, proclamations, and books. Whether he promoted an absolutism that upset the customary constitutional balance or merely reiterated a long-established theory of divine right that had its origins in the Middle Ages, James I arrived in England eager to assert his prerogatives, and in a speech to Parliament in

1610, he famously announced: "The state of monarchy is the supremest thing upon earth: for kings are not only God's lieutenants upon earth, and sit upon God's thrones, but even by God himself they are called gods." His immediate polemical aim in this speech was to preclude disputes about the king's prerogative and to counter resistance theories being promulgated by religious dissidents. Above all, especially in the wake of the Gunpowder Plot, James I was eager to preach the necessity of nonresistance. However, his attempt to undercut any religious justification for resistance invests the monarchy with a new sanctity: kings are not only "the supremest thing upon earth," they even seem to share God's divinity. Though divine right theories emerged in the Middle Ages in an effort to assert the independence of monarchy against the jurisdictional claims of the papacy, it was Henry VIII's break with the Church of Rome that made the theory a political reality. The Act in Restraint of Appeals to Rome (1533) famously declared, "this realm of England is an empire" and insisted that the English king was not subject to the Pope's authority. Consequently, the defenders of the English Reformation, including James I, sought to endow the English monarch, now the head of the English church, with a compelling sanctity to counter the claim that Holy Church had been subject to a violently political usurpation. If Shakespeare's contemporaries were confused and troubled about the sources of the sacred, James I sought to offer at least one clear answer: the king _is_ sacred, and obedience is the subject's first duty.

 Macbeth, however, does not provide obvious support for James I's theory of monarchy. Certainly there is great horror at the killing of a saintly king, an act that spreads disorder throughout the human and the natural world, but while the precise political institutions of _Macbeth_'s Scotland are never revealed, it is clear that Macbeth assumes the throne through a procedure of acclamation that at least initially confers legitimacy. It has frequently been pointed out that the play depicts a moment in Scottish history in which the royal succession was shifting from a system known as tanistry, whereby the succession was determined by the election of the eldest and worthiest among the surviving kinsmen of the deceased king, to the more familiar model of lineal succession through primogeniture. Though the play makes no direct reference to this change, the constitutional order remains murky. If inheritance by the eldest son was the accepted norm, then it is hard to understand the reason for Duncan's explicit nomination of Malcolm. The very act seems to imply that Malcolm's accession was neither inevitable nor expected, and indeed Macbeth's immediate reaction—"That is a step / On which I must fall down or else o'erleap, / For in my way it lies" (1.4.48–50)—suggests that he, too, sees it as a new development. While these constitutional uncertainties complicate the issue of legitimacy, there can be little question that the armed expedition that Malcolm leads into Scotland in order to defeat the tyrant is precisely the sort of action that James I condemned. James allowed that a king in "a settled kingdom leaves to be a king and degenerates into a tyrant as soon as he leaves off to rule according to his laws," and there is no doubt that in these terms Macbeth is a tyrant, but James also insists that even under such circumstances rebellion is not allowed. The tyrant must be left to his conscience and to God.

Perhaps most unsettling of all in political terms is the fact that Malcolm's investiture at Scone does not "trammel up the consequence" (1.7.3) of Macbeth's crime. There are too many loose threads, and the ending uncannily repeats the beginning. The play begins and ends in violence, but there is no reason to anticipate an end of violence. Indeed, according to Raphael Holinshed's *The Chronicles of England, Scotland, and Ireland* (1587), Shakespeare's historical source, Donalbain—who flees to Ireland in Act Two, scene three—later murders Malcolm's son. Moreover, the prediction concerning James I's ancestor Banquo, that he shall "get kings" (1.3.67), has yet to be fulfilled. The audience's knowledge that the offspring of Banquo, the progenitors of the present English King, will come, one way or another, to the throne makes Malcolm's success precarious. Despite Malcolm's evident political skill, there is little reason to think that the hurly-burly will end. Fleance, though he has "No teeth for th' present," (3.4.31) has escaped, and perhaps even more unsettling, the witches in all their inscrutable malevolence remain at large.

Shakespeare and His England
by David Scott Kastan

hakespeare is a household name, one of those few that don't need a first name to be instantly recognized. His first name was, of course, William, and he (and it, in its Latin form, *Gulielmus*) first came to public notice on April 26, 1564, when his baptism was recorded in the parish church of Stratford-upon-Avon, a small market town about ninety miles northwest of London. It isn't known exactly when he was born, although traditionally his birthday is taken to be April 23rd. It is a convenient date (perhaps too convenient) because that was the date of his death in 1616, as well as the date of St. George's Day, the annual feast day of England's patron saint. It is possible Shakespeare was born on the 23rd; no doubt he was born within a day or two of that date. In a time of high rates of infant mortality, parents would not wait long after a baby's birth for the baptism. Twenty percent of all children would die before their first birthday.

Life in 1564, not just for infants, was conspicuously vulnerable. If one lived to age fifteen, one was likely to live into one's fifties, but probably no more than 60 percent of those born lived past their mid-teens. Whole towns could be ravaged by epidemic disease. In 1563, the year before Shakespeare was born, an outbreak of plague claimed over one third of the population of London. Fire, too, was a constant threat; the thatched roofs of many houses were highly flammable, as well as offering handy nesting places for insects and rats. Serious crop failures in several years of the decade of the 1560s created food short-ages, severe enough in many cases to lead to the starvation of the elderly and the infirm, and lowering the resistances of many others so that between 1536 and 1560 influenza claimed over 200,000 lives.

Shakespeare's own family in many ways reflected these unsettling realities. He was one of eight children, two of whom did not survive their first year, one of whom died at age eight; one lived to twenty-seven, while the four surviving siblings died at ages ranging from Edmund's thirty-nine to William's own fifty-two years. William married at an unusually early age. He was only eighteen, though his wife was twenty-six, almost exactly the norm of the day for women, though men normally married also in their mid- to late twenties. Shakespeare's wife Anne was already pregnant at the time that the marriage was formally confirmed, and a daughter, Susanna, was born six months later, in May 1583. Two years later, she gave birth to twins, Hamnet and Judith. Hamnet would die in his eleventh year.

If life was always at risk from what Shakespeare would later call "the thousand natural shocks / That flesh is heir to" (*Hamlet*, 3.1.61–62), the incessant threats to peace were no less unnerving, if usually less immediately life threatening. There were almost daily rumors of foreign invasion and civil war as the Protestant Queen Eliz-abeth assumed the crown in 1558 upon the death of her Catholic half sister, Mary. Mary's reign had been marked by the public burnings of Protestant "heretics," by the seeming subordination of England to Spain, and by a commitment to a ruinous war with France, that, among its other effects, fueled inflation and encouraged a debasing of the currency. If, for many, Elizabeth represented the hopes for a peaceful and prosperous Protestant future, it seemed unlikely in the early days of her rule that the young monarch could hold her England together against the twin menace of the powerful Catholic monarchies of Europe and the significant part of her own population who were reluctant to give up their old faith. No wonder the Queen's principal secretary saw England in the early years of Elizabeth's rule as a land surrounded by "perils many, great and imminent."

In Stratford-upon-Avon, it might often have been easy to forget what threatened from without. The simple rural life, shared by about 90 percent of the English populace, had its reassuring natural rhythms and delights. Life was structured by the daily rising and setting of the sun, and by the change of seasons. Crops were planted and harvested; livestock was bred, its young delivered; sheep were sheared, some livestock slaughtered. Market days and fairs saw the produce and crafts of the town arrayed as people came to sell and shop—and be entertained by musicians, dancers, and troupes of actors. But even in Stratford, the lurking tensions and dangers could be daily sensed. A few months before Shakespeare was born, there had been a shocking "defacing" of images in the church, as workmen, not content merely to whitewash over the religious paintings decorating the interior as they were ordered, gouged large holes in those felt to be too "Catholic"; a few months after Shakespeare's birth, the register of the same church records another deadly outbreak of plague. The sleepy market town on the northern bank of the gently flowing river Avon was not immune from the menace of the world that surrounded it.

This was the world into which Shakespeare was born. England at his birth was still poor and backward, a fringe nation on the periphery of Europe. English itself was a minor language, hardly spoken outside of the country's borders. Religious tension was inescapable, as the old Catholic faith was trying determinedly to hold on, even as Protestantism was once again anxiously trying to establish itself as the national religion. The country knew itself vulnerable to serious threats both from without and from within. In 1562, the young Queen, upon whom so many people's hopes rested, almost fell victim to smallpox, and in 1569 a revolt of the Northern earls tried to remove her from power and restore Catholicism as the national religion. The following year, Pope Pius V pronounced the excommunication of "Elizabeth, the pretended queen of England" and forbade Catholic subjects obedience to the monarch on pain of their own excommunication. "Now we are in an evil way and going to the devil," wrote one clergyman, "and have all nations in our necks."

It was a world of dearth, danger, and domestic unrest. Yet it would soon dramatically change, and Shakespeare's literary contribution would, for future generations, come to be seen as a significant measure of England's remarkable transformation. In the course of Shakespeare's life, England, hitherto an unsophisticated and under-developed backwater acting as a bit player in the momentous political dramas taking place on the European continent, became a confident, prosperous, global presence. But this new world was only accidentally, as it is often known today, "The Age of Shakespeare." To the degree that historical change rests in the hands of any individual, credit must be given to the Queen. This new world arguably was "The Age of Elizabeth," even if it was not the Elizabethan Golden Age, as it has often been portrayed.

The young Queen quickly imposed her personality upon the nation. She had talented councilors around her, all with strong ties to her of friendship or blood, but the direction of government was her own. She was strong willed and cautious, certain of her right to rule and convinced that stability was her greatest responsibility. The result may very well have been, as historians have often charged, that important issues facing England were never dealt with head-on and left to her successors to settle, but it meant also that she was able to keep her England unified and for the most part at peace.

Religion posed her greatest challenge, though it is important to keep in mind that in this period, as an official at Elizabeth's court said, "Religion and the commonwealth cannot be parted asunder." Faith then was not the largely voluntary commitment it is today, nor was there any idea of some separation of church and state. Religion was literally a matter of life and death, of salvation and damnation, and the Church was the Church of England. Obedience to it was not only a matter of conscience but also of law. It was the single issue on which the nation was most likely to be torn apart.

Elizabeth's great achievement was that she was successful in ensuring that the Church of England became formally a Protestant Church, but she did so without either driving most of her Catholic subjects to sedition or alienating the more radical Protestant community. The so-called "Elizabethan Settlement" forged a broad Christian community of what has been called prayer-book Protestantism, even as many of its practitioners retained, as a clergyman said, "still a smack and savor of popish principles." If there were forces on both sides who were uncomfortable with the Settlement—committed Protestants, who wanted to do away with all vestiges of the old faith, and convinced Catholics, who continued to swear their allegiance to Rome—the majority of the country, as she hoped, found ways to live comfortably both within the law and within their faith. In 1571, she wrote to the Duke of Anjou that the forms of worship she recommended would "not properly compel any man to alter his opinion in the great matters now in controversy in the Church." The official toleration of religious ambiguity, as well as the familiar experience of an official change of state religion accompanying the crowning of a new monarch, produced a world where the familiar labels of Protestant and Catholic failed to define the forms of faith that most English people practiced. But for Elizabeth, most matters of faith could be left to individuals, as long as the Church itself, and Elizabeth's position at its head, would remain unchallenged.

In international affairs, she was no less successful with her pragmatism and willingness to pursue limited goals. A complex mix of prudential concerns about religion, the economy, and national security drove her foreign policy. She did not have imperial ambitions; in the main, she wanted only to be sure there would be no invasion of England and to encourage English trade. In the event, both goals brought England into conflict with Spain, determining the increasingly anti-Catholic tendencies of English foreign policy and, almost accidentally, England's emergence as a world power. When Elizabeth came to the throne, England was in many ways a mere satellite nation to the Netherlands, which was part of the Hapsburg Empire that the Catholic Philip II (who had briefly and unhappily been married to her predecessor and half sister, Queen Mary) ruled from Spain; by the end of her reign England was Spain's most bitter rival.

The transformation of Spain from ally to enemy came in a series of small steps (or missteps), no one of which was intended to produce what in the end came to pass. A series of posturings and provocations on both sides led to the rupture. In 1568, things moved to their breaking point, as the English confiscated a large shipment of gold that the Spanish were sending to their troops in the Netherlands. The following year saw the revolt of the Catholic earls in Northern England, followed by the papal excommunication of the Queen in 1570, both of which were by many in England assumed to be at the initiative, or at very least with the tacit support, of Philip. In fact he was not involved, but England under Elizabeth would never again think of Spain as a loyal friend or reliable ally. Indeed, Spain quickly became its mortal enemy. Protestant Dutch rebels had been opposing the Spanish domination of the Netherlands since the early 1560s, but, other than periodic financial support, Elizabeth had done little to encourage them. But in 1585, she sent troops under the command of the Earl of Leicester to support the Dutch rebels against the Spanish. Philip decided then to launch a full-scale attack on England, with the aim of deposing Elizabeth and restoring the Catholic faith. An English assault on Cadiz in 1587 destroyed a number of Spanish ships, postponing Philip's plans, but in the summer of 1588 the mightiest navy in the world, Philip's grand armada, with 132 ships and 30,493 sailors and troops, sailed for England.

By all rights, it should have been a successful invasion, but a combination of questionable Spanish tactics and a fortunate shift of wind resulted in one of England's greatest victories. The English had twice failed to intercept the armada off the coast of Portugal, and the Spanish fleet made its way to England, almost catching the English ships resupplying in Plymouth. The English navy was on its heels, when conveniently the Spanish admiral decided to anchor in the English Channel off the French port of Calais to wait for additional troops coming from the Netherlands. The English attacked with fireships, sinking four Spanish galleons, and strong winds from the south prevented an effective counterattack from the Spanish. The Spanish fleet was pushed into the North Sea, where it regrouped and decided its safest course was to attempt the difficult voyage home around Scotland and Ireland, losing almost half its ships on the way. For many in England the improbable victory was a miracle, evidence of God's favor for Elizabeth and the Protestant nation. Though war with Spain would not end for another fifteen years, the victory over the armada turned England almost overnight into a major world power, buoyed by confidence that they were chosen by God and, more tangibly, by a navy that could compete for control of the seas.

From a backward and insignificant Hapsburg satellite, Elizabeth's England had become, almost by accident, the leader of Protestant Europe. But if the victory over the armada signaled England's new place in the world, it hardly marked the end of England's travails. The economy, which initially was fueled by the military buildup, in the early 1590s fell victim to inflation, heavy taxation to support the war with Spain, the inevitable wartime disruptions of trade, as well as crop failures and a general economic downturn in Europe. Ireland, over which England had been attempting to impose its rule since 1168, continued to be a source of trouble and great expense (in some years costing the crown nearly one fifth of its total revenues). Even when the most organized of the rebellions, begun in 1594 and led by Hugh O'Neill, Earl of Tyrone, formally ended in 1603, peace and stability had not been achieved.

But perhaps the greatest instability came from the uncertainty over the succession, an uncertainty that marked Elizabeth's reign from its beginning. Her near death from smallpox in 1562 reminded the nation that an unmarried queen could not insure the succession, and Elizabeth was under constant pressure to marry and produce an heir. She was always aware of and deeply resented the pressure, announcing as early as 1559: "this shall be for me sufficient that a marble stone shall declare that a queen, having reigned such a time, lived and died a virgin." If, however, it was for her "sufficient," it was not so for her advisors and for much of the nation, who hoped she would wed. Arguably Elizabeth was the wiser, knowing that her unmarried hand was a political advantage, allowing her to diffuse threats or create alliances with the seeming possibility of a match. But as with so much in her reign, the strategy bought temporary stability at the price of longer-term solutions.

By the mid 1590s, it was clear that she would die unmarried and without an heir, and various candidates were positioning themselves to succeed her. Enough anxiety was produced that all published debate about the succession was forbidden by law. There was no direct descendant of the English crown to claim rule, and all the claimants had to reach well back into their family history to find some legitimacy. The best genealogical claim belonged to King James VI of Scotland. His mother, Mary, Queen of Scots, was the granddaughter of James IV of Scotland and Margaret Tudor, sister to Elizabeth's father, Henry VIII. Though James had right on his side, he was, it must be remembered, a foreigner. Scotland shared the island with England but was a separate nation. Great Britain, the union of England and Scotland, would not exist formally until 1707, but with Elizabeth's death early in the morning of March 24, 1603, surprisingly uneventfully the thirty-seven-year-old James succeeded to the English throne. Two nations, one king: King James VI of Scotland, King James I of England.

Most of his English subjects initially greeted the announcement of their new monarch with delight, relieved that the crown had successfully been transferred without any major disruption and reassured that the new King was married with two living sons. However, quickly many became disenchanted with a foreign King who spoke English with a heavy accent, and dismayed even further by the influx of Scots in positions of power. Nonetheless, the new King's greatest political liability may well have been less a matter of nationality than of temperament: he had none of Elizabeth's skill and ease in publicly wooing her subjects. The Venetian ambassador wrote back to the doge that the new King was unwilling to "caress the people, nor make them that good cheer the late Queen did, whereby she won their loves."

He was aloof and largely uninterested in the daily activities of governing, but he was interested in political theory and strongly committed to the cause of peace. Although a steadfast Protestant, he lacked the reflexive anti-Catholicism of many of his subjects. In England, he achieved a broadly consensual community of Protestants. The so-called King James Bible, the famous translation published first in 1611, was the result of a widespread desire to have an English Bible that spoke to all the nation, transcending the religious divisions that had placed three different translations in the hands of his subjects. Internationally, he styled himself *Rex Pacificus* (the peace-loving king). In 1604, the Treaty of London brought Elizabeth's war with Spain formally to an end, and over the next decade he worked to bring about political marriages that might cement stable alliances. In 1613, he married his daughter to the leader of the German Protestants, while the following year he began discussions with Catholic Spain to marry his son to the Infanta Maria. After some ten years of negotiations, James's hopes for what was known as the Spanish match were finally abandoned, much to the delight of the nation, whose long-felt fear and hatred for Spain outweighed the subtle political logic behind the plan.

But if James sought stability and peace, and for the most part succeeded in his aims (at least until 1618, when the bitter religio-political conflicts on the European continent swirled well out of the

King's control), he never really achieved concord and cohesion. He ruled over two kingdoms that did not know, like, or even want to understand one another, and his rule did little to bring them closer together. His England remained separate from his Scotland, even as he ruled over both. And even his England remained self divided, as in truth it always was under Elizabeth, ever more a nation of prosperity and influence but still one forged out of deep-rooted divisions of means, faiths, and allegiances that made the very nature of English identity a matter of confusion and concern. Arguably this is the very condition of great drama—sufficient peace and prosperity to support a theater industry and sufficient provocation in the troubling uncertainties about what the nation was and what fundamentally mattered to its people to inspire plays that would offer tentative solutions or at the very least make the troubling questions articulate and moving.

Nine years before James would die in 1625, Shakespeare died, having returned from London to the small market town in which he was born. If London, now a thriving modern metropolis of well over 200,000 people, had, like the nation itself, been transformed in the course of his life, the Warwickshire market town still was much the same. The house in which Shakespeare was born still stood, as did the church in which he was baptized and the school in which he learned to read and write. The river Avon still ran slowly along the town's southern limits. What had changed was that Shakespeare was now its most famous citizen, and, although it would take more than another 100 years to fully achieve this, he would in time become England's, for having turned the great ethical, social, and political issues of his own age into plays that would live forever.

William Shakespeare: A Chronology

1558	**November 17: Queen Elizabeth crowned**
1564	April 26: Shakespeare baptized, third child born to John Shakespeare and Mary Arden
1564	**May 27: Death of Jean Calvin in Geneva**
1565	John Shakespeare elected alderman in Stratford-upon-Avon
1568	**Publication of the Bishops' Bible**
1568	September 4: John Shakespeare elected Bailiff of Stratford-upon-Avon
1569	**Northern Rebellion**
1570	**Queen Elizabeth excommunicated by the Pope**
1572	**August 24: St. Bartholomew's Day Massacre in Paris**
1576	**The Theatre is built in Shoreditch**
1577–1580	**Sir Francis Drake sails around the world**
1582	November 27: Shakespeare and Anne Hathaway married (Shakespeare is 18)
1583	Queen's Men formed
1583	May 26: Shakespeare's daughter, Susanna, baptized
1584	**Failure of the Virginia Colony**

1585   February 2: Twins, Hamnet and Judith, baptized (Shakespeare is 20)

1586   Babington Plot to dethrone Elizabeth and replace her with Mary, Queen of Scots

1587   February 8: Execution of Mary, Queen of Scots

1587   Rose Theatre built

1588   August: Defeat of the Spanish armada (Shakespeare is 24)

1588   September 4: Death of Robert Dudley, Earl of Leicester

1590   First three books of Spenser's *Faerie Queene* published; Marlowe's *Tamburlaine* published

1592   March 3: *Henry VI, Part One* performed at the Rose Theatre (Shakespeare is 27)

1593   February–November: Theaters closed because of plague

1593   Publication of *Venus and Adonis*

1594   Publication of *Titus Andronicus*, first play by Shakespeare to appear in print (though anonymously)

1594   Lord Chamberlain's Men formed

1595   March 15: Payment made to Shakespeare, Will Kemp, and Richard Burbage for performances at court in December, 1594

1595   Swan Theatre built

1596   Books 4–6 of *The Faerie Queene* published

1596   August 11: Burial of Shakespeare's son, Hamnet (Shakespeare is 32)

1596–1599   Shakespeare living in St. Helen's, Bishopsgate, London

1596   October 20: Grant of Arms to John Shakespeare

1597   May 4: Shakespeare purchases New Place, one of the two largest houses in Stratford (Shakespeare is 33)

1598   Publication of *Love's Labor's Lost*, first extant play with Shakespeare's name on the title page

1598   Publication of Francis Meres's *Palladis Tamia*, citing Shakespeare as "the best for Comedy and Tragedy" among English writers

1599   **Opening of the Globe Theatre**

1601   **February 7: Lord Chamberlain's Men paid 40 shillings to play *Richard II* by supporters of the Earl of Essex, the day before his abortive rebellion**

1601   **February 17: Execution of Robert Devereaux, Earl of Essex**

1601   September 8: Burial of John Shakespeare

1602   May 1: Shakespeare buys 107 acres of farmland in Stratford

1603   **March 24: Queen Elizabeth dies; James VI of Scotland succeeds as James I of England** (Shakespeare is 39)

1603   May 19: Lord Chamberlain's Men reformed as the King's Men

1604   Shakespeare living with the Mountjoys, a French Huguenot family, in Cripplegate, London

1604   **First edition of Marlowe's *Dr. Faustus* published (written c. 1589)**

1604   March 15: Shakespeare named among "players" given scarlet cloth to wear at royal procession of King James

1604   Publication of authorized version of *Hamlet* (Shakespeare is 40)

1605   **Gunpowder Plot**

1605   June 5: Marriage of Susanna Shakespeare to John Hall

1608   Publication of *King Lear* (Shakespeare is 44)

1608–1609   Acquisition of indoor Blackfriars Theatre by King's Men

1609   *Sonnets* published

1611   **King James Bible published** (Shakespeare is 47)

1612   **November 6: Death of Henry, eldest son of King James**

1613   **February 14: Marriage of King James's daughter Elizabeth to Frederick, the Elector Palatine**

1613   March 10: Shakespeare, with some associates, buys gatehouse in Blackfriars, London

1613   **June 29: Fire burns the Globe Theatre**

1614   **Rebuilt Globe reopens**

1616   February 10: Marriage of Judith Shakespeare to Thomas Quiney

1616   March 25: Shakespeare's will signed

1616   April 23: Shakespeare dies (age 52)

1616   **April 23: Cervantes dies in Madrid**

1616   April 25: Shakespeare buried in Holy Trinity Church in Stratford-upon-Avon

1623   August 6: Death of Anne Shakespeare

1623   **October: Prince Charles, King James's son, returns from Madrid, having failed to arrange his marriage to Maria Anna, Infanta of Spain**

1623   First Folio published with 36 plays (18 never previously published)

Words, Words, Words: Understanding Shakespeare's Language
by David Scott Kastan

t is silly to pretend that it is easy to read Shakespeare. Reading Shakespeare isn't like picking up a copy of *USA Today* or *The New Yorker*, or even F. Scott Fitzgerald's *Great Gatsby* or Toni Morrison's *Beloved*. It is hard work, because the language is often unfamiliar to us and because it is more concentrated than we are used to. In the theater it is usually a bit easier. Actors can clarify meanings with gestures and actions, allowing us to get the general sense of what is going on, if not every nuance of the language that is spoken. "Action is eloquence," as Volumnia puts it in *Coriolanus*, "and the eyes of th' ignorant / More learnèd than the ears" (3.276–277). Yet the real greatness of Shakespeare rests not on "the general sense" of his plays but on the specificity and suggestiveness of the words in which they are written. It is through language that the plays' full dramatic power is realized, and it is that rich and robust language, often pushed by Shakespeare to the very limits of intelligibility, that we must learn to understand. But we can come to understand it (and enjoy it), and this essay is designed to help.

Even experienced readers and playgoers need help. They often find that his words are difficult to comprehend. Shakespeare sometimes uses words no longer current in English or with meanings that have changed. He regularly multiplies words where seemingly one might do as well or even better. He characteristically writes sentences that are syntactically complicated and imaginatively dense. And it isn't just we, removed by some 400 years from his world, who find him difficult to read; in his own time, his friends and fellow actors knew Shakespeare was hard. As two of them, John Hemings and Henry Condell, put it in their prefatory remarks to Shakespeare's First Folio in 1623, "read him, therefore, and again and again; and if then you do not like him, surely you are in some manifest danger not to understand him."

From the very beginning, then, it was obvious that the plays both deserve and demand not only careful reading but continued re-reading—and that not to read Shakespeare with all the attention a reader can bring to bear on the language is almost to guarantee that a reader will not "understand him" and remain among those who "do not like him." But Shakespeare's colleagues were nonetheless confident that the plays exerted an attraction strong enough to ensure and reward the concentration of their readers, confident, as they say, that in them "you will find enough, both to draw and hold you." The plays do exert a kind of magnetic pull, and have successfully drawn in and held readers for over 400 years.

Once we are drawn in, we confront a world of words that does not always immediately yield its delights; but it will—once we learn to see what is demanded of us. Words in Shakespeare do a lot, arguably more than anyone else has ever asked them to do. In part, it is because he needed his words to do many things at once. His stage had no sets and few props, so his words are all we have to enable us to imagine what his characters see. And they also allow us to see what the characters don't see, especially about themselves. The words are vivid and immediate, as well as complexly layered and psychologically suggestive. The difficulties they pose are not the "thee's" and "thou's" or "prithee's" and "doth's" that obviously mark the chronological distance between Shakespeare and us. When

Gertrude says to Hamlet, "thou hast thy father much offended" (3.4.8), we have no difficulty understanding her chiding, though we might miss that her use of the "thou" form of the pronoun expresses an intimacy that Hamlet pointedly refuses with his reply: "Mother, *you* have my father much offended" (3.4.9; italics mine).

Most deceptive are words that look the same as words we know but now mean something different. Words often change meanings over time. When Horatio and the soldiers try to stop Hamlet as he chases after the Ghost, Hamlet pushes past them and says, "I'll make a ghost of him that lets me" (1.4.85). It seems an odd thing to say. Why should he threaten someone who "lets" him do what he wants to do? But here "let" means "hinder," not, as it does today, "allow" (although the older meaning of the word still survives, for example, in tennis, where a "let serve" is one that is hindered by the net on its way across). There are many words that can, like this, mislead us: "his" sometimes means "its," "an" often means "if," "envy" means something more like "malice," "cousin" means more generally "kinsman," and there are others, though all are easily defined. The difficulty is that we may not stop to look thinking we already know what the word means, but in this edition a ° following the word alerts a reader that there is a gloss in the left margin, and quickly readers get used to these older meanings.

Then, of course, there is the intimidation factor—strange, polysyllabic, or Latinate words that not only are foreign to us but also must have sounded strange even to Shakespeare's audiences. When Macbeth wonders whether all the water in all the oceans of the world will be able to clean his bloody hands after the murder of Duncan, he concludes: "No; this my hand will rather / The multitudinous seas incarnadine, / Making the green one red" (2.2.64–66). Duncan's blood staining Macbeth's murderous hand is so offensive that, not merely does it resist being washed off in water, but it will "the multitudinous seas incarnadine": that is, turn the sea-green oceans blood-red. Notes will easily clarify the meaning of the two odd words, but it is worth observing that they would have been as odd to Shakespeare's readers as they are to us. The *Oxford English Dictionary* (*OED*) shows no use of "multitudinous" before this, and it records no use of "incarnadine" before 1591 (*Macbeth* was written about 1606). Both are new words, coined from the Latin, part of a process in Shakespeare's time where English adopted many Latinate words as a mark of its own emergence as an important vernacular language. Here they are used to express the magnitude of Macbeth's offense, a crime not only against the civil law but also against the cosmic order, and then the simple monosyllables of turning "the green one red" provide an immediate (and needed) paraphrase and register his own sickening awareness of the true hideousness of his deed.

As with "multitudinous" in *Macbeth*, Shakespeare is the source of a great many words in English. Sometimes he coined them himself, or, if he didn't invent them, he was the first person whose writing of them has survived. Some of these words have become part of our language, so common that it is hard to imagine they were not always part of it: for example, "assassination" (*Macbeth*, 1.7.2), "bedroom" (*A Midsummer Night's Dream*, 2.2.57), "countless" (*Titus Andronicus*, 5.3.59), "fashionable" (*Troilus and Cressida*, 3.3.165), "frugal" (*The Merry Wives of Windsor*, 2.1.28), "laughable" (*The Merchant of Venice*, 1.1.56), "lonely" (*Coriolanus*, 4.1.30), and "useful" (*King John*, 5.2.81). But other words that he originated were not as, to use yet another Shakespearean coinage, "successful" (*Titus Andronicus*, 1.1.66). Words like "crimeless" (*Henry VI, Part Two*, 2.4.63, meaning "innocent"), "facinorous" (*All's Well That Ends Well*, 2.3.30, meaning "extremely wicked"), and "recountment" (*As You Like It*, 4.3.141, meaning "narrative" or "account") have, without much resistance, slipped into oblivion. Clearly Shakespeare liked words, even unwieldy ones. His working vocabulary, about 18,000 words, is staggering, larger than almost any other English writer, and he seems to be the first person to use in print about

1,000 of these. Whether he coined the new words himself or was intrigued by the new words he heard in the streets of London doesn't really matter; the point is that he was remarkably alert to and engaged with a dynamic language that was expanding in response to England's own expanding contact with the world around it.

But it is neither new words nor old ones that are the source of the greatest difficulty of Shakespeare's language. The real difficulty (and the real delight) comes in trying to see how he uses the words, how he endows them with more than their denotative meanings. Why, for example, does Macbeth say that he hopes that the "sure and firm-set earth" (2.1.56) will not hear his steps as he goes forward to murder Duncan? Here "sure" and "firm-set" mean virtually the same thing: stable, secure, fixed. Why use two words? If this were a student paper, no doubt the teacher would circle one of them and write "redundant." But the redundancy is exactly what Shakespeare wants. One word would do if the purpose were to describe the solidity of the earth, but here the redundancy points to something different. It reveals something about Macbeth's mind, betraying through the doubling how deep is his awareness of the world of stable values that the terrible act he is about to commit must unsettle.

Shakespeare's words usually work this way: in part describing what the characters see and as often betraying what they feel. The example from *Macbeth* is a simple example of how this works. Shakespeare's words are carefully patterned. How one says something is every bit as important as what is said, and the conspicuous patterns that are created alert us to the fact that something more than the words' lexical sense has been put into play. Words can be coupled, as in the example above, or knit into even denser metaphorical constellations to reveal something about the speaker (which often the speaker does not know), as in Prince Hal's promise to his father that he will outdo the rebels' hero, Henry Percy (Hotspur):

Percy is but my factor, good my lord,
To engross up glorious deeds on my behalf.
And I will call him to so strict account
That he shall render every glory up,
Yea, even the slightest worship of his time,
Or I will tear the reckoning from his heart.

(*Henry IV, Part One, 3.2.147–152*)

The Prince expresses his confidence that he will defeat Hotspur, but revealingly in a reiterated language of commercial exchange ("factor," "engross," "account," "render," "reckoning") that tells us something important both about the Prince and the ways in which he understands his world. In a play filled with references to coins and counterfeiting, the speech demonstrates not only that Hal has committed himself to the business at hand, repudiating his earlier, irresponsible tavern self, but also that he knows it is a business rather than a glorious world of chivalric achievement; he inhabits a world in which value (political as well as economic) is not intrinsic but determined by what people are willing to invest, and he proves himself a master of producing desire for what he has to offer.

Or sometimes it is not the network of imagery but the very syntax that speaks, as when Claudius announces his marriage to Hamlet's mother:

Therefore our sometime sister, now our Queen,
Th' imperial jointress to this warlike state,
Have we—as 'twere with a defeated joy,
With an auspicious and a dropping eye,
With mirth in funeral and with dole in marriage,
In equal scale weighing delight and dole—
Taken to wife.   (*Hamlet, 1.2.8–14*)

All he really wants to say here is that he has married Gertrude, his former sister-in-law: "Therefore our sometime sister . . . Have we . . . Taken to wife." But the straightforward sentence gets interrupted and complicated, revealing his own discomfort with the announcement. His elaborations and intensifications of Gertrude's role ("sometime sister," "Queen," "imperial jointress"), the self-conscious rhetorical balancing of the middle three lines (indeed "in equal scale weighing delight and dole"), all declare by the all-too obvious artifice how desperate he is to hide the awkward facts behind a veneer of normalcy and propriety. The very unnaturalness of the sentence is what alerts us that we are meant to understand more than the simple relation of fact.

Why doesn't Shakespeare just say what he means? Well, he does—exactly what he means. In the example from *Hamlet* just above, Shakespeare shows us something about Claudius that Claudius doesn't know himself. Always Shakespeare's words will offer us an immediate sense of what is happening, allowing us to follow the action, but they also offer us a counterplot, pointing us to what might be behind the action, confirming or contradicting what the characters say. It is a language that shimmers with promise and possibility, opening the characters' hearts and minds to our view—and all we have to do is learn to pay attention to what is there before us.

Shakespeare's Verse

Another distinctive feature of Shakespeare's dramatic language is that much of it is in verse. Almost all of the plays mix poetry and prose, but the poetry dominates. *The Merry Wives of Windsor* has the lowest percentage (only about 13 percent verse), while *Richard II* and *King John* are written entirely in verse (the only examples, although *Henry VI, Part One* and *Part Three* have only a very few prose lines). In most of the plays, about 70 percent of the lines are written in verse.

Shakespeare's characteristic verse line is a non-rhyming iambic pentameter ("blank verse"), ten syllables with every second one stressed. In *A Midsummer Night's Dream*, Titania comes to her senses after a magic potion has led her to fall in love with an ass-headed Bottom: "Methought I was enamored of an ass" (4.1.76). Similarly, in *Romeo and Juliet*, Romeo gazes up at Juliet's window: "But soft, what light through yonder window breaks" (2.2.2). In both these examples, the line has ten syllables organized into five regular beats (each beat consisting of the stress on the second syllable of a pair, as in "But soft," the da-dum rhythm forming an "iamb"). Still, we don't hear these lines as jingles; they seem natural enough, in large part because this dominant pattern is varied in the surrounding lines.

The play of stresses indeed becomes another key to meaning, as Shakespeare alerts us to what is important. In *Measure for Measure*, Lucio urges Isabella to plead for her brother's life: "Oh, to him, to him, wench! He will relent" (2.2.129). The iambic norm (unstressed-stressed) tells us (and an actor) that the emphasis at the beginning of the line is on "to" not "him"—it is the action not the object that is being emphasized—and at the end of the line the stress falls on "will." Alternatively, the line can play against the established norm. In *Hamlet*, Claudius corrects Polonius's idea of what is bothering the Prince: "Love? His affections do not that way tend" (3.1.161). The iambic norm forces the emphasis onto "that" ("do not *that* way tend"), while the syntax forces an unexpected stress on the opening word, "Love." In the famous line, "The course of true love never did run smooth" (*A Midsummer Night's Dream*, 1.1.134), the iambic expectation is varied in both the middle and at the end of the line. Both "love" and the first syllable of "never" are stressed, as are both syllables at the end: "run smooth," creating a metrical foot in which both syllables are stressed (called a "spondee"). The point to notice is that the "da-dum, da-dum, da-dum, da-dum, da-dum" line is not inevitable; it merely sets an expectation against which many variations can be heard.

In fact, even the ten-syllable norm can be varied. Shakespeare sometimes writes lines with fewer or more syllables. Often there is an extra, unstressed syllable at the end of a line (a so-called "feminine ending"); sometimes there are verse lines with only nine. In *Henry IV, Part One*, King Henry replies incredulously to the rebel Worcester's claim that he hadn't "sought" the confrontation with the King: "You have not sought it. How comes it then?" (5.1.27). There are only nine syllables here (some earlier editors, seeking to "correct" the verse, added the word "sir" after the first question to regularize the line). But the pause where one expects a stressed syllable is dramatically effective, allowing the King's anger to be powerfully present in the silence.

As even these few examples show, Shakespeare's verse is unusually flexible, allowing a range of rhythmical effects. It should not be understood as a set of strict rules but as a flexible set of practices rooted in dramatic necessity. It is designed to highlight ideas and emotions, and it is based less upon rigid syllable counts than on an arrangement of stresses within an understood temporal norm, as one might expect from a poetry written to be heard in the theater rather than read on the page.

Here Follows Prose

Although the plays are dominated by verse, prose plays a significant role. Shakespeare's prose has its own rhythms, but it lacks the formal patterning of verse, and so is printed without line breaks and without the capitals that mark the beginning of a verse line. Like many of his fellow dramatists, Shakespeare tended to use prose for comic scenes, the shift from verse serving, especially in his early plays, as a social marker. Upper-class characters speak in verse; lower-class characters speak in prose. Thus, in *A Midsummer Night's Dream*, the Athenians of the court, as well as the fairies, all speak in verse, but the "rude mechanicals," Bottom and his artisan friends, all speak in prose, except for the comic verse they speak in their performance of "Pyramis and Thisbe."

As Shakespeare grew in experience, he became more flexible about the shifts from verse to prose, letting it, among other things, mark genre rather than class and measure various kinds of intensity. Prose becomes in the main the medium of comedy. The great comedies, like *Much Ado About Nothing*, *Twelfth Night*, and *As You Like It*, are all more than 50 percent prose. But even in comedy, shifts between verse and prose may be used to measure subtle emotional changes. In Act One, scene three of *The Merchant of Venice*, Shylock and Bassanio begin the scene speaking of matters of business in prose, but when Antonio enters and the deep conflict between the Christian and the Jew becomes evident, the scene shifts to verse. But prose may itself serve in moments of emotional intensity. Shylock's famous speech in Act Three, scene one, "Hath not a Jew eyes . . ." is all in prose, as is Hamlet's expression of disgust at the world ("I have of late— but wherefore I know not—lost all my mirth . . .") at 3.1.261–276. Shakespeare comes to use prose to vary the tone of a scene, as the shift from verse subtly alerts an audience or a reader to some new emotional register.

Prose becomes, as Shakespeare's art matures, not inevitably the mark of the lower classes but the mark of a salutary daily-ness. It is appropriately the medium in which letters are written, and it is the medium of a common sense that will at least challenge the potential self-deceptions of grandiloquent speech. When Rosalind mocks the excesses and artifice of Orlando's wooing in Act Four, scene one of *As You Like It*, it is in prose that she seeks something genuine in the expression of love:

> The poor world is almost six thousand years old, and in all this time there was not any man died in his own person, *videlicit* [i.e., namely], in a love cause. . . . Men have died from time to time, and worms have eaten them, but not for love.

Here the prose becomes the sound of common sense, an effective foil to the affectation of pinning poems to trees and thinking that it is real love.

It is not that prose is artless; Shakespeare's prose is no less self-conscious than his verse. The artfulness of his prose is different, of course. The seeming ordinariness of his prose is no less an effect of his artistry than is the more obvious patterning of his verse. Prose is no less serious, compressed, or indeed figurative. As with his verse, Shakespeare's prose performs numerous tasks and displays various, subtle formal qualities; and recognizing the possibilities of what it can achieve is still another way of seeing what Shakespeare puts right before us to show us what he has hidden.

Further Reading

N.F. Blake, *Shakespeare's Language: An Introduction* (New York: St. Martin's Press, 1983).

Jonathan Hope, *Shakespeare's Grammar* (London: Thomson, 2003).

Sister Miriam Joseph, *Shakespeare's Use of the Arts of Language* (New York: Columbia University Press, 1947).

M. M. Mahood, *Shakespeare's Wordplay* (London: Methuen, 1957).

Russ McDonald, *Shakespeare and the Arts of Language* (Oxford: Oxford University Press, 2001).

Brian Vickers, *The Artistry of Shakespeare's Prose* (London: Methuen, 1968).

George T. Wright, *Shakespeare's Metrical Art* (Berkeley: Univ. of California Press, 1991).

Key to the Play Text

Symbols

o   Indicates an explanation or definition in the
             left-hand margin.

1   Indicates a gloss on the page facing the play text.

[]   Indicates something added or changed by the editors
             (i.e., not in the early printed text that this edition
             of the play is based on).

Terms

F, Folio, or   The first collected edition of Shakespeare's plays,
First Folio   published in 1623.

Q, Quarto   The usual format in which the individual plays were
             first published.

Macbeth

William Shakespeare

List of Roles

Duncan	King of Scotland
Malcolm }	his sons
Donalbain }	
Macbeth	Thane of Glamis, later Thane of Cawdor, later King of Scotland
Lady Macbeth	his wife, later Queen of Scotland
Porter	at Macbeth's castle
Seyton	an officer serving Macbeth
Gentlewoman	serving Lady Macbeth
Banquo	a Scottish thane
Fleance	his son
Macduff	Thane of Fife
Lady Macduff	his wife
Son	their child
Lennox	
Ross	
Mentieth }	Scottish thanes
Angus	
Caithness	
Siward	Earl of Northumberland
Young Siward	his son
Lord	
English Doctor	
Scottish Doctor	
Captain	in Duncan's army
Old Man	
Three Murderers of Banquo	
Murderers at Macduff's Castle	
Messenger	
Messenger	
Servant to Macbeth	
Servant to Lady Macbeth	
Three Witches	the weird sisters
Hecate	
Three Other Witches	
Three Apparitions	

Lords, gentlemen, soldiers, officers, attendants, messengers, a sewer, servants

1   *Graymalkin / Paddock*

Graymalkin was a common name for
a domestic cat, and a *paddock* is a
toad or frog. Both creatures are
spirit "familiars" who perform
magical tasks for the witches.
Familiars were a prominent part of
English witch lore.

Act 1, Scene 1

Thunder and lightning.

Enter three **Witches**.

[handwritten: connection to the greek Fates 3 (the weird sisters)]

First Witch

[handwritten: at end of this meeting]

When shall we three meet again? *[handwritten: question]*

In thunder, lightning, or in rain?

[handwritten: what R they meeting about]

Second Witch

[handwritten: battle – scots vs. Norwigians, trivial to them, war is childs game]

turmoil is

When the hurly-burly's° done,

When the battle's lost and won.

Third Witch

before

That will be ere° the set of sun.   5

[handwritten: dont care game to them]

First Witch

Where the place?

Second Witch

Upon the heath.

Third Witch

There to meet with Macbeth.

First Witch

I come, Graymalkin!

[handwritten: ommous – tension – what R they going to do w/ him]

Second Witch

Paddock¹ calls.

Third Witch

Right away

Anon.°   10

All

[handwritten: appearances are decieving]

Fair is foul, and foul is fair.

Hover through the fog and filthy air.   *They exit.*

1   Alarum

    Signal to arms

2   within

    **I.e., offstage. In the
    amphitheaters where
    Shakespeare's plays were first
    performed, the offstage area
    consisted primarily of the *tiring-
    house*, a large room behind the
    backstage wall where actors
    changed their costumes. There
    were no offstage wings on the left
    or right, as in modern indoor
    theaters.**

3   *As seemeth by his plight*

    I.e., judging by his wounds

4   *As two spent swimmers that do cling
    together / And choke their art*

    **Like exhausted swimmers who, by
    holding on to each other, are both
    unable to use their skill (*art*) in
    swimming**

5   *to that*

    **As if to that end (i.e., in order to
    make Macdonwald a rebel)**

6   *The multiplying villanies of nature / Do
    swarm upon him*

    **(1) Macdonwald attracts
    increasingly large numbers of
    villainous individuals to his
    rebellion, like swarming flies;
    (2) Macdonwald's villainous
    qualities swarm around him as
    they multiply.**

7   *Western Isles*

    **Probably the Hebrides, islands off
    the northwest coast of Scotland,
    but *kerns and gallowglasses* (see
    below) also suggest Ireland**

8   *kerns and gallowglasses*

    **Types of Irish soldiers; *kerns* were
    light-armed Irish foot soldiers
    (*OED*), and *gallowglasses* refers to
    horsemen armed with axes.**

9   *fortune, on his damnèd quarry smiling*

    **His most likely refers to
    Macdonwald, though it might refer
    to *fortune*, who has created this
    battle. (Fortune was usually
    personified as female, but *his* could
    be used for "her.") Some editions
    emend *quarry* to *quarrel* (which
    appears in the source passage in
    Holinshed); the use of *quarry*
    suggests that Macdonwald is
    ultimately doomed to be fortune's
    prey, while *quarrel* suggests, more
    simply, that fortune momentarily
    favored his cause.**

10 *smoked with bloody execution*

    I.e., was so bloody it gave off steam

11 *Which ne'er shook hands, nor bade
    farewell to him*

    **I.e., Macdonwald refrained from
    the usual courtesies of chivalric
    warfare, refusing to shake hands
    with or greet Macbeth.**

Act 1, Scene 2

Alarum [1] within. [2] Enter **King** [**Duncan**], **Malcolm**, (Duncan's sons)

Donalbain, [*and*] **Lennox**, *with attendants, meeting*

a bleeding **Captain**. (Scottish Thane)

(in Duncan's army)

Duncan (King of Scotland)

What bloody man is that? He can report,

As seemeth by his plight, [3] of the revolt

condition   The newest state.°

Malcolm (King's son)

officer   This is the sergeant°

Who like a good and hardy soldier fought

'Gainst my captivity. —Hail, brave friend!   5

battle   Say to the King the knowledge of the broil°

As thou didst leave it.

Captain

              Doubtful it stood,

exhausted   As two spent° swimmers that do cling together

And choke their art. [4] The merciless Macdonwald—

Worthy to be a rebel, for to that [5]   10

The multiplying villanies of nature

Do swarm upon him [6]—from the Western Isles [7]

Of kerns and gallowglasses [8] is supplied,

And fortune, on his damnèd quarry smiling, [9]

appeared   Showed° like a rebel's whore. But all's too weak,   15

For brave Macbeth—well he deserves that name—

Disdaining fortune, with his brandished steel,

Which smoked with bloody execution, [10]

favorite   Like valor's minion,° carved out his passage

i.e., Macdonwald   Till he faced the slave,°   20

Who   Which° ne'er shook hands, nor bade farewell to him, [11]

1 *unseamed him from the nave to th' chops*
Cut him open from the navel to the jaw

2 *fixed his head upon*
Placed Macdonwald's severed head on

3 *As whence the sun 'gins his reflection / Shipwracking storms and direful thunders break, / So from that spring whence comfort seemed to come / Discomfort swells.*
Just as the spring equinox brings with it stormy weather, the apparent success in defeating Macdonwald brings on another battle.

4 *furbished*
Polished, hence not yet used

5 *as sparrows eagles, or the hare the lion*
As much as sparrows dismay eagles, or hares dismay lions (i.e., not at all)

6 *As cannons overcharged with double cracks, / So they doubly redoubled strokes upon the foe*
I.e., Macbeth and Banquo fought even more strongly than before, like cannons with twice their normal charge of gunpowder.

7 *memorize another Golgotha*
Create a scene as memorable as Golgotha, the site where Jesus was crucified.

Till he unseamed him from the nave to th' chops[1]
And fixed his head upon[2] our battlements.

[handwritten margin note: Macbeth war hero – killed Rebel Macdonwald]

Duncan (King)

kinsman   O valiant cousin!° Worthy gentleman!

Captain

As whence the sun 'gins his reflection   25
Shipwracking storms and direful thunders break,
So from that spring whence comfort seemed to come

Note; listen carefully   Discomfort swells.[3] Mark,° King of Scotland, mark:
No sooner justice had, with valor armed,

fleeing; fearful   Compelled these skipping° kerns to trust their heels,   30

his opportunity   But the Norweyan lord, surveying vantage,°
With furbished[4] arms and new supplies of men
Began a fresh assault.

Duncan (King)

Dismayed not this our captains, Macbeth and Banquo?

Captain

Yes, as sparrows eagles, or the hare the lion.[5]   35

truth   If I say sooth,° I must report they were
As cannons overcharged with double cracks,
So they doubly redoubled strokes upon the foe.[6]

Whether   Except° they meant to bathe in reeking wounds,
Or memorize another Golgotha,[7]   40
I cannot tell—
But I am faint; my gashes cry for help.

Duncan (King)

So well thy words become thee as thy wounds;
They smack of honor both. Go get him surgeons.

                              [**Captain** *exits with attendants.*]

            Enter **Ross** and **Angus**.
                (Scottish Thanes)

Who comes here?   .

1   *Thane*

A Scottish landowner and head of
a clan, owing obedience only to
the king

2   *So should he look / That seems to speak*
things strange.

That is how someone who is
about to say strange things looks.

3   *Till that Bellona's bridegroom*

Until the husband of Bellona,
Roman goddess of war (i.e.,
Macbeth)

4   *lapped in proof*

Sheathed in armor

5   *with self-comparisons*

With equal prowess in battle

6   *Point against point*

Sword point against sword point;
in every detail

7   *Saint Colme's Inch*

Inchcolm, an island (named for
St. Columba) in the Firth (estuary)
of Forth, near Edinburgh. *Colme's*
is pronounced "kol-lums."

8   *dollars*

German silver coins (actually
thalers) used in the 16th century,
five centuries after the play is
supposed to have taken place.

9   *Our bosom interest*

Our most intimate concern (*our* is
used here as a royal pronoun);
i.e., both Duncan's and Scotland's
interest.

10   *with his former title greet Macbeth*

Tell Macbeth he is now the Thane
of Cawdor.

Malcolm (King's son)

                The worthy Thane [1] of Ross.   45

Lennox (Scottish Thane)

is visible   What a haste looks° through his eyes. So should he look

That seems to speak things strange. [2]

Ross (Scottish Thane)

                  God save the King.

Duncan (King)

Whence cam'st thou, worthy Thane?

Ross (Thane)

                  From Fife, great King,

insult   Where the Norweyan banners flout° the sky

And fan our people cold.   50

i.e., The King of Norway   Norway° himself, with terrible numbers,

Assisted by that most disloyal traitor,

The Thane of Cawdor, began a dismal conflict,

Till that Bellona's bridegroom, [3] lapped in proof, [4]

Confronted him with self-comparisons, [5]   55

Point against point, [6] rebellious arm 'gainst arm,

wild   Curbing his lavish° spirit; and, to conclude,

The victory fell on us.

Duncan (King)

        Great happiness!

Ross (Thane)

                That now Sweno,

Norwegians'/a truce   The Norways'° king, craves composition.°

Nor would we deign him burial of his men   60

Till he disbursèd at Saint Colme's Inch [7]

Ten thousand dollars [8] to our general use.

Duncan (King)

No more that Thane of Cawdor shall deceive

imminent   Our bosom interest. [9] Go pronounce his present° death

And with his former title greet Macbeth. [10]   65

Ross (Thane)
I'll see it done.
Duncan (King)
What he hath lost, noble Macbeth hath won.   *They exit.*

Macbeth - praised
of success in battle -
becomes Thane of Cawdor

1   *Killing swine.*

Witches were frequently accused
of harming farm animals. The vast
majority of English witchcraft
prosecutions concerned these
sorts of putative malicious
enchantments.

2   *Aroint thee*

Begone; the word *aroint* seems
unique to Shakespeare at this time.

3   *rump-fed runnion*

Lecherous woman

4   Tiger

Name of the husband's ship;
contemporary accounts of travel to
Africa and the Middle East refer to a
voyage to Tripoli (and later Aleppo,
by caravan) on a ship called the *Tiger*.

5   *in a sieve I'll thither sail*

That she could sail in a sieve would
demonstrate a witch's power. This
colorful detail finds a striking
parallel in the accounts of the
Berwick witches in Scotland in
1590–1591. Famously, King James
was involved in the interrogation
and prosecution of these witches,
who were accused of having
attempted to kill him with
enchantments. In *Newes from
Scotland* (1592), the witches are
described as sailing on the sea in
sieves.

6   *a rat without a tail*

It was commonly thought that
witches could transform
themselves into the shape of any
four-footed beast, but, lacking the
corresponding body part, they
would necessarily be tailless.

7   *all the other, / And the very ports they
blow, / All the quarters that they know /
I' th' shipman's card*

All the other winds, as well as the
ports from which the winds blow
(preventing the ship from docking)
and all the directions that the
sailor's charts (*card*) can find.

8   *penthouse lid*

I.e., eyelid; a *penthouse* was a small
shelter with a sloped roof.

Act 1, Scene 3

Thunter. Enter the three **Witches**. (Weird The sisters)

First Witch

Where hast thou been, sister?

Second Witch

Killing swine. [1]

Third Witch

Sister, where thou?

First Witch

A sailor's wife had chestnuts in her lap
And munched, and munched, and munched. "Give
   me," quoth I.   5
"Aroint thee, [2] witch!" the rump-fed runnion [3] cries.

(a Syrian city) Her husband's to Aleppo° gone, master o' th' *Tiger*; [4]
But in a sieve I'll thither sail, [5]

in the shape of And like° a rat without a tail, [6]

act; fornicate I'll do,° I'll do, and I'll do.   10

Second Witch

I'll give thee a wind.

First Witch

Th' art kind.

Third Witch

And I another.

First Witch

I myself have all the other,
And the very ports they blow,   15
All the quarters that they know
I' th' shipman's card. [7]
I'll drain him dry as hay.
Sleep shall neither night nor day
Hang upon his penthouse lid. [8]   20

1 *sev'nnights nine times nine*
I.e., eighty-one weeks

2 *lost*
Made to disappear; perhaps
destroyed

3 *weird*
The Folio spelling is consistently
"weyward" (1.3.32, 1.5.8, 2.1.25) or
"weyard" (3.1.2, 3.4.134, 4.1.158),
both of which are plausible early
spellings for *wayward* (cf. 3.5.11), an
appropriate association for the
willful and unruly sisters.
Nonetheless, it seems the
intended word is the modern
"weird" (which could be itself, in
Shakespeare's time, spelled
"wayward"). *Weird* derives from the
Old English *Wyrd*, meaning fate or
destiny, and it was often used to
describe the three classical Fates.
Holinshed's *Chronicles of Scotland*,
Shakespeare's source, reports that
Macbeth and Banquo met "three
women in strange and wild
apparel, resembling creatures of
elder world." Holinshed adds,
"common opinion was that these
women were either the weird
sisters, that is (as ye would say) the
goddesses of destiny, or else some
nymphs or fairies, endowed with
knowledge of prophesy by their
necromantical science."
Holinshed's "as ye would say"
indicates that the word was
unfamiliar, and a later account by

Peter Heylyn mentions "three
Fairies, or Witches (*Weirds* the *Scots*
call them)" suggesting that the word
was marked as foreign. Though the
play's speech prefixes and stage
directions refer to witches, they are
always called the *weird sisters* by
Macbeth and Banquo.

4 *Posters*
Fast travelers

5 *wound up*
I.e., ready. The familiar idiom,
usually applied to the strings of a
musical instrument, was already
applied to springs and watches
when the play was written.

6 *Forres*
A Scottish town east of Inverness.
The Folio prints "Soris," seemingly
misreading an "f" as a long "s."

accursed   He shall live a man forbid.°
             Weary sev'nnights nine times nine[1]
waste away   Shall he dwindle, peak,° and pine.
ship   Though his bark° cannot be lost,[2]
               Yet it shall be tempest-tossed.   25
               Look what I have.

Second Witch

Show me; show me.

First Witch

Here I have a pilot's thumb,
Wrecked   Wracked° as homeward he did come.   *Drum within.*

Third Witch

A drum, a drum!   30
Macbeth doth come.

All

The weird[3] sisters, hand in hand,
Posters[4] of the sea and land,
Thus do go about, about,
Thrice to thine and thrice to mine   35
And thrice again to make up nine.
Peace! The charm's wound up.[5]

Enter **Macbeth** *and* **Banquo**. (scottish Thane)
                                              a
                                          (Thane of Glamis,
Macbeth   later Thane of Cawdor, later
                                                  King of
So foul and fair a day I have not seen.   Scotland)

Banquo (Scottish Thane)

estimated to be   How far is 't called° to Forres?[6]—What are these,
                    So withered and so wild in their attire,   40

1 *Glamis*

An area in Tayside, in northeast
Scotland, pronounced as the
meter demands, either "Glahms"
or "Glah-miss."

2 *fantastical*

Imaginary, i.e., existing only in
Macbeth's and Banquo's minds

3 *with present grace and great prediction /*
Of noble having and of royal hope, /
That he seems rapt withal

By his already held title (Thane of
Glamis) and with predictions of
gaining a new title (Cawdor) and
also the throne, so that he seems
dazed by all the news

That look not like th' inhabitants o' th' Earth

And yet are on 't?—Live you? Or are you aught

speak with   That man may question?° You seem to understand me,

chapped   By each at once her choppy° finger laying

appear to   Upon her skinny lips. You should° be women,   45

And yet your beards forbid me to interpret

That you are so.

Macbeth

               Speak, if you can: what are you?

First Witch

All hail, Macbeth! Hail to thee, Thane of Glamis! [1]

Second Witch

All hail, Macbeth! Hail to thee, Thane of Cawdor!

Third Witch

All hail, Macbeth, that shalt be king hereafter!   50

Banquo

Good sir, why do you start and seem to fear

Things that do sound so fair? [*to* **Witches**] I' th' name of

    truth,

Are ye fantastical, [2] or that indeed

appear   Which outwardly ye show?° My noble partner

You greet with present grace and great prediction   55

Of noble having and of royal hope,

That he seems rapt withal. [3] To me you speak not.

If you can look into the seeds of time

And say which grain will grow and which will not,

Speak then to me, who neither beg nor fear   60

Your favors nor your hate.

First Witch

Hail!

Second Witch

Hail!

1 *imperfect speakers*

Ambiguous prophecies were a
common literary motif in
Shakespeare's time. In *The Arte of
English Poesie* (1589), George
Puttenham discusses them as
instances of verbal ambiguity in
general, citing the prophecies of
the famous Oracle at Delphi of
ancient Greece as examples of
ambiguous speech devised to
"abuse the superstitious people."
Puttenham observes that similarly
unclear prophecies have
frequently "stirred up" rebellions
in England. In *2 Henry VI* (1.4),
Shakespeare depicts an
ambiguous oracle that proves true,
but in *King Lear* the Fool offers a
paradoxical prophecy that seems
to parody the very idea of such
predictions (3.2.81–94).

2 *Sinel's death*

The death of Sinel, Macbeth's father
(though historically his name was
Finel.) Shakespeare follows the error
in Holinshed, no doubt resulting
from misreading an "f" as a long "s."
See 1.3.39 and note.

3 *from whence / You owe*

Where you got

4 vanish

The Globe amphitheater, where
most of Shakespeare's plays were
originally performed, had several
means of making the witches
vanish, including trapdoors and
smoke. In the indoor theaters, they
might "fly" away, lifted by hoists.

Third Witch

Hail!

First Witch

Lesser than Macbeth and greater.   65

Second Witch

fortunate   Not so happy,° yet much happier.

Third Witch

beget   Thou shalt get° kings, though thou be none.

So all hail Macbeth and Banquo!

First Witch

Banquo and Macbeth, all hail!

Macbeth

inexplicit   Stay, you imperfect° speakers; [1] tell me more.   70

By Sinel's death [2] I know I am Thane of Glamis,

 hɪs dad   But how of Cawdor? The Thane of Cawdor lives,

A prosperous gentleman, and to be king

scope   Stands not within the prospect° of belief,

No more than to be Cawdor. Say from whence   75

information   You owe [3] this strange intelligence,° or why

desolate; blighted   Upon this blasted° heath you stop our way

With such prophetic greeting. Speak, I charge you.

Witches vanish. [4]

Banquo (Thane)

The earth hath bubbles, as the water has,

And these are of them. Whither are they vanished?   80

Macbeth

corporeal   Into the air, and what seemed corporal°

I wish   Melted, as breath into the wind. Would° they had
stayed.

1   *eaten on the insane root*

Eaten of the root that causes
madness (probably one of many
narcotic roots such as hemlock or
henbane)

2   *To th' selfsame tune and words.*

I.e., that is exactly what they said.

3   *His wonders and his praises do contend /*
Which should be thine or his

The clause is obscure, but the
general sense is that Macbeth's
actions are so astonishing that if
the King gives in to his amazement
he will be too dumbstruck to voice
his praise, but in order to praise
Macbeth he must first deny his
own astonishment.

4   *Silenced with that, / . . . / He finds thee*
in the stout Norweyan ranks, / Nothing
afeard of what thyself didst make, /
Strange images of death.

Silenced by his wonder and
admiration, he learns that you
fought the Norwegians as well as
the rebels, not at all afraid of the
forms of death that you yourself
inflicted (but the language
ironically anticipates Macbeth's
treason by placing him *in the stout*
Norweyan ranks).

5   *As thick as tale / Came post with post*

Messengers came as quickly as
they could be counted; *tale* here
means "count or list." Some
editions (following Rowe in 1709)
change this to *As thick as hail / Came*
post with post. The change makes
the lines slightly easier to
interpret, but the sense of
numerous messages coming
quickly stands.

Banquo (Th an e)

Were such things here as we do speak about,
Or have we eaten on the insane root[1]
That takes the reason prisoner?   85

Macbeth

Your children shall be kings.

Banquo (Thane)

                                        You shall be king.

Macbeth

And Thane of Cawdor too: went it not so?

Banquo (Thane)

To th' selfsame tune and words.[2] Who's here?

Enter **Ross** *and* **Angus**.

Ross (Scottish Thane)

The King hath happily received, Macbeth,
considers   The news of thy success, and when he reads°   90
risk   Thy personal venture° in the rebels' fight,
His wonders and his praises do contend
Which should be thine or his.[3] Silenced with that,
In viewing o'er the rest o' th' selfsame day,
valiant   He finds thee in the stout° Norweyan ranks,   95
Nothing afeard of what thyself didst make,
forms   Strange images° of death.[4] As thick as tale
Came post with post,[5] and every one did bear
Thy praises in his kingdom's great defense,
And poured them down before him.

Angus (Scottish Thane)

                                        We are sent   100
To give thee from our royal master thanks,
Only to herald thee into his sight,
Not pay thee.

1 *can the devil speak true?*

The force of Banquo's question
depends on the proverbial
understanding that the devil is the
father of lies (cf. John 8:44).
Banquo's comment in lines 123–
126, that the devil sometimes
speaks the truth, is also proverbial.
This is a point that comes up
repeatedly in the literature on
demonology and witchcraft. For
example, Lewis Lavater, in *Of
Ghostes and Spirites Walking by Nyght*
(1572), explains that "Devils do
sometimes bid men those things
which are good, and avoid things
that are evil: sometimes they tell
truth." Lavater emphatically rejects
the argument that "those Spirits
speak truth, but the Devil is a liar,
and is called so by Christ the father
of lies. Therefore we may not say
that they are devilish Spirits."
Shakespeare's *Hamlet* raises this
very problem: the truth of the
apparition's accusation against
Claudius does not establish that it
is a spirit of health.

2 *Whether he was combined / With those
of Norway, or did line the rebel / With
hidden help and vantage, or that with
both / He labored in his country's wrack*

Whether he was allied with Norway
or conspiring with Macdonwald, or
with both enemies labored to
defeat his country

3 *The greatest is behind*

Either "the larger number of titles
(i.e., Glamis and Cawdor) is already
achieved," or, more likely, "the
greatest is still to come" (i.e., the
crown).

4 *That, trusted home, / Might yet enkindle
you unto the crown*

That sort of thinking, fully
embraced, might encourage your
hopes for the crown. *Enkindle*
literally means "cause to blaze";
here it implies fiery excitement
and passion.

5 *win us to our harm*

Charm us into participating in our
destruction

Ross *(Thane)*

anticipation; pledge And, for an earnest° of a greater honor,

He bade me, from him, call thee Thane of Cawdor: 105

title In which addition,° hail, most worthy Thane,

For it is thine.

Banquo *(Thane)*

What, can the devil speak true? [1]

Macbeth

The Thane of Cawdor lives. Why do you dress me

In borrowed robes?

Angus *(Thane)*

He who Who° was the Thane lives yet,

But under heavy judgment bears that life 110

Which he deserves to lose. Whether he was combined

reinforce With those of Norway, or did line° the rebel

benefit With hidden help and vantage,° or that with both

He labored in his country's wrack, [2] I know not;

deserving death But treasons capital,° confessed and proved, 115

Have overthrown him.

Macbeth

[*aside*] Glamis, and Thane of Cawdor!

The greatest is behind. [3] [*to* **Ross** *and* **Angus**] Thanks for
   your pains.

[*aside to* **Banquo**] Do you not hope your children shall
   be kings,

When those that gave the Thane of Cawdor to me

Promised no less to them?

Banquo *(Thane)*

entirely That, trusted home,° 120

Might yet enkindle you unto the crown, [4]

Besides the Thane of Cawdor. But 'tis strange.

And oftentimes, to win us to our harm, [5]

The instruments of darkness tell us truths,

1 *prologues to the swelling act*

Macbeth uses theatrical terms to describe this progress toward the throne.

2 *that suggestion / Whose horrid image doth unfix my hair / And make my seated heart knock at my ribs*

I.e., the notion of killing Duncan, the image of which causes my hair to stand on end and my heart to pound in my chest.

3 *Present fears / Are less than horrible imaginings.*

Fearful things that are actually present are less frightening than imagined horrors.

4 *My thought, whose murder yet is but fantastical, / Shakes so my single state of man / That function is smothered in surmise*

The phrasing is distorted as Macbeth unconsciously allows the idea of murder to creep into his language. The possessive adjective *whose* modifies *murder* but it does not reveal clearly who or what is being murdered and by whom. Usually *thought* is interpreted as the yet unrealized (but *fantastical*) thought of killing Duncan, an anticipation that powerfully disrupts Macbeth's undivided condition of honesty and integrity (*my single state of man*) and impedes his ability to perform proper actions (*function*) in the present.

5 *If chance will have me king, why, chance may crown me / Without my stir.*

In Shakespeare's source, Holinshed's *Chronicles*, Macbeth decides to wait before acting in the hope that "divine providence" would work to make him king, just as it made him Thane of Cawdor. By replacing Holinshed's "divine providence" with *chance*, Shakespeare removes the suggestion that Macbeth imagines secular affairs to be entirely in the control of God.

6 *New honors come upon him / Like our strange garments, cleave not to their mold / But with the aid of use.*

His new offices, like new clothes, will not fit him comfortably until he becomes used to them.

us	Win us with honest trifles, to betray 's°	125

In deepest consequence.

[*to* **Ross** *and* **Angus**] Cousins, a word, I pray you.

Macbeth

[*aside*] Two truths are told,

As happy prologues to the swelling act ¹

Of the imperial theme. [*to* **Ross** *and* **Angus**] I thank you,

gentlemen.   130

incitement; temptation [*aside*] This supernatural soliciting°

evil Cannot be ill,° cannot be good. If ill,

pledges Why hath it given me earnest° of success,

Commencing in a truth? I am Thane of Cawdor.

If good, why do I yield to that suggestion   135

Whose horrid image doth unfix my hair

And make my seated heart knock at my ribs ²

custom Against the use° of nature? Present fears

Are less than horrible imaginings. ³

My thought, whose murder yet is but fantastical,   140

composed; unitary Shakes so my single° state of man

That function is smothered in surmise, ⁴

And nothing is but what is not.

Banquo (Thane)

Look how our partner's rapt.

Macbeth

[*aside*] If chance will have me king, why, chance may

crown me   145

Without my stir. ⁵

Banquo (Thane)

                              New honors come upon him,

Like our strange garments, cleave not to their mold

But with the aid of use. ⁶

1   *Come what come may, / Time and the*
    hour runs through the roughest day.
    I.e., "whatever happens will
    happen." The second line means,
    more specifically, "time keeps
    going, even through the toughest
    times."

2   *your pains / Are registered where every*
    day I turn / The leaf to read them
    I.e., I have recorded your help (in
    my memory) as if in a journal.

Macbeth

                      [*aside*] Come what come may,
Time and the hour runs through the roughest day. [1]

Banquo (Thane)

wait   Worthy Macbeth, we stay° upon your leisure.   150

Macbeth

indulgence / occupied   Give me your favor.° My dull brain was wrought°
With things forgotten. Kind gentlemen, your pains
Are registered where every day I turn
The leaf to read them. [2] Let us toward the King.

taken place   [*aside to* **Banquo**] Think upon what hath chanced,° and,

after   at° more time,   155

In the   The° interim having weighed it, let us speak

open; honest   Our free° hearts each to other.

Banquo (Thane)

                     Very gladly.

Macbeth

Till then, enough. [*to* **Ross** *and* **Angus**] Come, friends.

                              They exit.

1   Flourish

Fanfare (a set of trumpet notes announcing the presence of the King)

2   *Those in commission*

I.e., those commissioned to execute Cawdor

3   *As one that had been studied in his death*

I.e., as though he had practiced or prepared for his death

4   *There's no art / To find the mind's construction in the face.*

I.e., there's no way to discern a person's inner character from an outward appearance. The idea that one cannot read the mind by looking at the face is proverbial. "Faces are not to be trusted" (*frontis nulla fides*) is a famous Latin motto written by the Roman poet Juvenal in his *Satire* 2. Shakespeare's contemporary, the poet Geoffrey Whitney, uses Juvenal's motto as the caption for an emblem (a pictorial representation of an abstract idea) in *Choice of Emblems* (1586). According to Whitney, unlike beasts that do not hide their violent inclinations, "man is made of such a seemly shape / That friend or foe is not discerned by face; / Then hard it is the wickeds' wiles to scape, / Since that the bad do mask with honest grace." Compare to 4.3.23–24.

5   *Thou art so far before, / That swiftest wing of recompense is slow / To overtake thee.*

I.e., you have gone so far ahead (of my ability to reward you) that whatever I offered would be inadequate.

6   *Would thou hadst less deserved, / That the proportion both of thanks and payment / Might have been mine.*

I.e., I wish you deserved less, so that I might be able adequately to reward you.

Act 1, Scene 4

Flourish. [1] *Enter* **King [Duncan], Lennox, Malcolm,** *← (King's son)*

Donalbain, *and attendants.* *(Scottish Thane)*

(King's son)

Duncan *(King)*

or are   Is execution done on Cawdor, or° not

Those in commission [2] yet returned?

Malcolm *(King's son)*

lord   My liege,°

They are not yet come back. But I have spoke

With one that saw him die, who did report

That very frankly he confessed his treasons,   5

Implored your Highness' pardon, and set forth

A deep repentance. Nothing in his life

Reflected so well on   Became° him like the leaving it. He died

As one that had been studied in his death [3]

owned   To throw away the dearest thing he owed°   10

unregarded   As 'twere a careless° trifle.

Duncan *(King)*

                          There's no art

To find the mind's construction in the face. [4]

He was a gentleman on whom I built

An absolute trust.

                 Enter **Macbeth, Banquo, Ross,** *and* **Angus.**

                     [*to* **Macbeth**] O worthiest cousin,

The sin of my ingratitude even now   15

ahead   Was heavy on me. Thou art so far before°

That swiftest wing of recompense is slow

To overtake thee. [5] Would thou hadst less deserved,

That the proportion both of thanks and payment

Only this   Might have been mine. [6] Only° I have left to say,   20

73

1   *by doing everything / Safe toward*
    By doing anything we can to
    protect

2   *establish our estate upon*
    Appoint as my successor. At the
    time the play is supposed to have
    taken place, the Scottish crown did
    not usually pass to the king's eldest
    son, but rather passed to a relative
    in a parallel family line (so a
    nephew usually succeeded his
    uncle), according to what was
    known as the law of tanistry.

3   *Prince of Cumberland*
    Title designating the heir to the
    Scottish throne. (See LONGER NOTE,
    page 291.)

4   *which honor must / Not unaccompanied*
    invest him only, / But signs of nobleness,
    like stars, shall shine / On all deservers
    Malcolm's honor will not be the
    only one bestowed; all deserving
    persons will receive their due

5   *Inverness*
    The site of Macbeth's castle; a town
    about 150 miles northwest of
    Edinburgh.

More is thy due than more than all can pay.

Macbeth

  The service and the loyalty I owe

role In doing it pays itself. Your Highness' part°

  Is to receive our duties, and our duties

  Are to your throne and state, children and servants,   25

only Which do but° what they should by doing everything

  Safe toward ¹ your love and honor.

Duncan (King)

           Welcome hither.

  I have begun to plant thee and will labor

  To make thee full of growing. —Noble Banquo,

  That hast no less deserved nor must be known   30

embrace No less to have done so, let me enfold° thee

  And hold thee to my heart.

Banquo (Thane)

         There, if I grow,

  The harvest is your own.

Duncan (King)

         My plenteous joys,

Profuse Wanton° in fullness, seek to hide themselves

  In drops of sorrow. Sons, kinsmen, thanes,   35

i.e., closest to the throne And you whose places are the nearest,° know

  We will establish our estate upon ²

  Our eldest, Malcolm, whom we name hereafter

  The Prince of Cumberland, ³ which honor must

adorn Not unaccompanied invest° him only,   40

  But signs of nobleness, like stars, shall shine

  On all deservers. ⁴ [to Macbeth] From hence to Inverness, ⁵

  And bind us further to you.

1   *The rest is labor which is not used for you*

(1) relaxation would seem a
hardship if it weren't in your
service; (2) anything (*the rest*) not
done in your service is work

2   *harbinger*

Messenger sent ahead to procure
lodgings, especially for royalty

3   *The eye wink at the hand, yet let that be /*
Which the eye fears, when it is done, to see.

Let the eye ignore the hand's
actions, yet let that thing happen
which the eye is appalled to see.

4   *full so valiant*

Fully as valiant (as Banquo has
presumably just said Macbeth is)

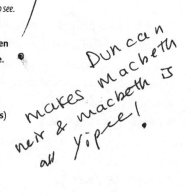

Duncan makes Macbeth heir & macbeth is all yipee!

Macbeth

The rest is labor which is not used for you: [1]
I'll be myself the harbinger [2] and make joyful   45
The hearing of my wife with your approach,
So humbly take my leave.

Duncan (King)

                              My worthy Cawdor!

Macbeth

[aside] The Prince of Cumberland! That is a step
On which I must fall down or else o'erleap,
For in my way it lies. Stars, hide your fires;   50
Let not light see my black and deep desires.
The eye wink at the hand, yet let that be
Which the eye fears, when it is done, to see. [3]   He exits.

Duncan (King)

True, worthy Banquo. He is full so valiant, [4]
And in his commendations I am fed;   55
It is a banquet to me. Let's after him,
Whose care is gone before to bid us welcome.

He   It° is a peerless kinsman.   Flourish. They exit.

1   *the perfect'st report*

The most reliable information.
However, notice that Macbeth
addresses them as *imperfect speakers*
in 1.3.70.

2   *lose the dues of rejoicing*

(1) miss the proper amount of
celebration; (2) lose time which
could be spent in rejoicing

3   *milk of human kindness*

The Folio reads "humane,"
though, until the 18th century,
"humane" and "human" could be
used interchangeably to indicate
either the species and its attributes
(reason, speech, and bipedality) or
"gentle" or marked by a sympathy
with and consideration for others.
Cf. *humane statute* (3.4.76). Here the
primary meaning seems to be
human as we presently use it. The
whole phrase is further
complicated by the dual senses of
kindness which can mean either
"benevolence" or a natural
tendency. The two words, *human
kindness*, then, could be read
together as "humankind," or,
alternatively, they could refer to a
kindly benevolence. In the first
sense, Lady Macbeth is only
recognizing that Macbeth is bound
by a sense of humanity (the very
humanity that she herself
renounces in 1.5.39–49). In the second,
she is accusing her husband of an
exaggerated sentimental concern.
The milk metaphor begins a series
of images that link lactation and
nursing with a normal supportive
humanity, and against which Lady
Macbeth's actions are set. She
invites invisible spirits to suck gall
instead of milk from her breasts
(1.5.47); later she claims that she
would kill *the babe that milks me*
before wavering as Macbeth has
done (1.7.55). Cf. *sweet milk of concord*
(4.3.98).

4   *To catch the nearest way*

To act in the most direct manner

5   *What thou wouldst highly, / That
wouldst thou holily*

Those great things you intensely
hope for, you want to attain in an
ethical way (*highly* = intensely, but
also carries the sense of Macbeth's
ambition)

6   *Thou 'ld'st have, great Glamis, / That which
cries, "Thus thou must do" if thou have it, / And
that which rather thou dost fear to do / Than
wishest should be undone.*

Lady Macbeth conspicuously
avoids actually naming the two
fundamental notions she
discusses in these phrases—that
is, Macbeth gaining the throne and
his murdering Duncan to get it.

7   *pour my spirits in thine ear*

I.e., transfer my spirit, or courage,
to you.

Act 1, Scene 5

Enter [**Lady Macbeth**] *alone, with a letter.*

Lady Macbeth (Macbeth's wife)

[*reading*] "They met me in the day of success, and I have
learned by the perfect'st report[1] they have more in
them than mortal knowledge. When I burned in desire
to question them further, they made themselves air,
into which they vanished. Whiles I stood rapt in the   5

messengers   wonder of it came missives° from the King, who all-
hailed me 'Thane of Cawdor,' by which title, before,
these weird sisters saluted me, and referred me to the
coming on of time with 'Hail, king that shalt be!' This

inform   have I thought good to deliver° thee, my dearest part-   10
ner of greatness, that thou might'st not lose the dues
of rejoicing[2] by being ignorant of what greatness is
promised thee. Lay it to thy heart, and farewell."
Glamis thou art and Cawdor, and shalt be

doubt   What thou art promised. Yet do I fear° thy nature.   15
It is too full o' th' milk of human kindness[3]
To catch the nearest way:[4] thou wouldst be great,
Art not without ambition, but without

wickedness   The illness° should attend it. What thou wouldst highly,
That wouldst thou holily;[5] wouldst not play false   20
And yet wouldst wrongly win. Thou 'ld'st have, great
     Glamis,

would have   That which cries, "Thus thou must do" if thou have° it,
And that which rather thou dost fear to do

Hasten   Than wishest should be undone.[6] Hie° thee hither,
That I may pour my spirits in thine ear[7]   25
And chastise with the valor of my tongue

crown   All that impedes thee from the golden round,°

1   *were 't so, / Would have informed for*
    preparation
    **If it were so, he would have
    notified us to prepare**

2   *had the speed of*
    Outran

3   *raven*
    **A bird of bad omen; the raven's
    croak was thought to signify
    impending death.**

4   *tend on mortal thoughts*
    **Respond to human (though also
    murderous) deliberation**

5   *compunctious visitings of nature*
    Natural feelings of compassion

6   *keep peace between / Th' effect and it*
    **Prevent any struggle between the
    consequences and my intention
    (i.e., don't let the fear of what may
    follow prevent me from acting)**

Macbeth & lady macbeths reactions to macbeth becoming heir greatly contrast - he feels bad about it she DOES not

supernatural Which fate and metaphysical° aid doth seem

with   To have thee crowned withal.°

                    Enter [a **Servant**].

news   What is your tidings?°

Servant

The King comes here tonight.

Lady Macbeth

                              Thou 'rt mad to say it.   30

Is not thy master with him, who, were 't so,

Would have informed for preparation?[1]

Servant

So please you, it is true: our Thane is coming.

One of my fellows had the speed of[2] him,

Who, almost dead for breath, had scarcely more   35

Than would make up his message.

Lady Macbeth

                              Give him tending.

He brings great news.   [**Servant**] *exits.*

                    The raven[3] himself is hoarse

deadly; fateful That croaks the fatal° entrance of Duncan

Under my battlements. Come, you spirits

That tend on mortal thoughts,[4] unsex me here   40

top of the head And fill me from the crown° to the toe top-full

Of direst cruelty. Make thick my blood.

compassion Stop up th' access and passage to remorse,°

That no compunctious visitings of nature[5]

terrible Shake my fell° purpose, nor keep peace between   45

Th' effect and it![6] Come to my woman's breasts

1   *take my milk for gall*
    **Replace my milk with *gall*, or bile.
    An excess of bile in the body was
    thought to cause envy and hatred.**

2   *wait on nature's mischief*
    Accompany natural disasters

3   *pall thee in the dunnest smoke of hell*
    **Envelop yourself in the darkest
    smoke of Hell (addressed to the
    thick night).**

4   *Greater than both, by the all-hail hereafter*
    **According to the weird sisters' *all-
    hail hereafter (All hail, Macbeth, that
    shalt be king hereafter*, 1.3.50),
    Macbeth will eventually gain a
    greater title than either Thane of
    Glamis or Thane of Cawdor.**

5   *To beguile the time, / Look like the time*
    **To deceive everyone, make your
    facial expression appropriate to
    the moment.**

agents   And take my milk for gall, [1] you murd'ring ministers,°
invisible   Wherever in your sightless° substances
    You wait on nature's mischief. [2] Come, thick night,
    And pall thee in the dunnest smoke of hell, [3]   50
    That my keen knife see not the wound it makes,
    Nor Heaven peep through the blanket of the dark
Stop   To cry "Hold;° hold!"

Enter **Macbeth.**

                Great Glamis, worthy Cawdor,
    Greater than both, by the all-hail hereafter, [4]
    Thy letters have transported me beyond   55
    This ignorant present, and I feel now
    The future in the instant.

Macbeth

                My dearest love,
    Duncan comes here tonight.

Lady Macbeth

                And when goes hence?

Macbeth

intends   Tomorrow, as he purposes.°

Lady Macbeth

                Oh, never
    Shall sun that morrow see!   60
    Your face, my Thane, is as a book where men
    May read strange matters. To beguile the time,
    Look like the time: [5] bear welcome in your eye,
    Your hand, your tongue. Look like th' innocent flower,
    But be the serpent under 't. He that's coming   65
    Must be provided for, and you shall put
management   This night's great business into my dispatch,°

1 *look up clear*

Keep your expression calm

2 *To alter favor ever is to fear.*

A change of expression (*favor*)
always invites suspicion and is
therefore to be feared (but also
suggests: "Fear is always likely to
alter one's expression").

Which shall to all our nights and days to come

us alone Give solely° sovereign sway and masterdom.

Macbeth

We will speak further.

Lady Macbeth

                             Only look up clear. [1]   70

To alter favor ever is to fear. [2]

Leave all the rest to me.   *They exit.*

1 Hautboys

Wooden, double-reed instruments, similar to the modern oboe.

2 *temple-haunting martlet*

Martin, a bird that often nests in churches. Banquo's subsequent lines indicate that a martin has managed to nest in the castle, attesting to Inverness's *delicate air.*

3 *coign of vantage*

Convenient corner

4 *pendant bed and procreant cradle*

The bird's suspended nest is both a bed for resting and a place for procreation.

5 *The love / That follows us sometime is our trouble, / Which still we thank as love.*

I.e., the love that we receive may sometimes seem bothersome, but we nonetheless remain thankful for that love.

6 *Herein I teach you / How you shall bid God 'ild us for your pains / And thank us for your trouble.*

I.e., you should see from this example how to ask God to reward me for your efforts, and you should thank me for causing you this trouble. Duncan's tone here is hard to gauge, oscillating between pretension, politeness, and self-deprecating irony.

7 *For those of old*

Because of the honors you have previously bestowed upon us

Act 1, Scene 6

Hautboys [1] *and torches. Enter* **King** [**Duncan**], **Malcolm,** ←(king's son)

(king's son)→ **Donalbain, Banquo, Lennox, Macduff, Ross,** son)

Angus, *and attendants* (thanes)(thane of Fife) (thane)

(thanes)

Duncan (king)

location   This castle hath a pleasant seat.° The air

Nimbly and sweetly recommends itself

Unto our gentle senses.

Banquo (thane)

             This guest of summer,

prove   The temple-haunting martlet, [2] does approve,°

i.e., nest-building   By his loved mansionry,° that the heaven's breath   5

projection   Smells wooingly here. No jutty,° frieze,

Buttress, nor coign of vantage, [3] but this bird

Hath made his pendant bed and procreant cradle. [4]

Where they most breed and haunt, I have observed,

The air is delicate.   10

Enter **Lady** [**Macbeth**].

Duncan (king)

See, see, our honored hostess! The love

That follows us sometime is our trouble,

Which still we thank as love. [5] Herein I teach you

yield (i.e., reward)   How you shall bid God 'ild° us for your pains

And thank us for your trouble. [6]

Lady Macbeth

             All our service,   15

detail   In every point° twice done and then done double,

would be / trivial   Were° poor and single° business to contend

with which   Against those honors deep and broad wherewith°

Your Majesty loads our house. For those of old, [7]

1   *We rest your hermits*
    **We remain bound to pray for you
    (*hermits* = beadsmen, religious men
    who pray on behalf of others,
    bound by vows or paid for the
    prayers).**

2   *coursed him at the heels*
    Were right behind him

3   *had a purpose / To be his purveyor*
    **Intended to arrive before him (a
    purveyor was a royal retainer who
    makes advance preparations for a
    king's visit)**

4   *Your servants ever / Have theirs, them-
    selves, and what is theirs in compt, / To
    make their audit at your Highness'
    pleasure, / Still to return your own.*
    **Your servants always consider their
    family members, themselves, and
    all their belongings as on loan
    from you, and are always ready to
    return them at your request.**

5   *By your leave*
    With your permission

recent   And the late° dignities heaped up to them,   20
We rest your hermits. [1]
Duncan (King)
                          Where's the Thane of Cawdor?
We coursed him at the heels [2] and had a purpose
To be his purveyor, [3] but he rides well,
helped   And his great love, sharp as his spur, hath holp° him
To his home before us. Fair and noble hostess,   25
We are your guest tonight.
Lady Macbeth

                          Your servants ever
Have theirs, themselves, and what is theirs in compt,
To make their audit at your Highness' pleasure,
Still to return your own. [4]
Duncan (King)
                          Give me your hand;
Bring   Conduct° me to mine host. We love him highly   30
And shall continue our graces towards him.
By your leave, [5] hostess.   *They exit.*

1   sewer and divers servants
    Steward and various servants

2   *If it were done when 'tis done, then*
    'twere well / It were done quickly.
    If this business would be finished
    when the murder was done, then it
    would be best to do it right away.
    Notice the reiterated *it* **as Macbeth**
    is unable to name the act.

3   *If th' assassination / Could trammel up*
    the consequence and catch / With his
    surcease success
    I.e., if the assassination would only
    effect my accession to the throne,
    (and tie up, as in a net, the trail of
    consequences), and with Duncan's
    death achieve my success

4   *bank and shoal*
    The Folio reads "Banke and
    Schoole," a pair of words with a
    number of interpretive possibilities.
    "Banke" could mean bench, the seat
    of justice, a sum of money, or the
    shop of a money dealer; "Schoole,"
    though a possible spelling of *shoal,*
    might mean school. Since benches
    were common in schools, the
    association makes sense, and seeing
    time as a place of instruction nicely
    anticipates *teach* **and** *instructions*
    (lines 8–9). The modernization here
    perhaps deprives the phrase of its
    full resonance; nonetheless ,the
    result is a familiar metaphor that

presents time as a river: Macbeth
stands either at the river's bank or
on a shoal in the midst of the river.

5   *jump the life to come*
    Risk (but see LONGER NOTE, **page 291)**

6   *We still have judgment here, that we but*
    teach / Bloody instructions, which, being
    taught, return / To plague th' inventor
    We still face consequences here on
    Earth, because our crimes have
    taught others how to act against us.

7   *Hath borne his faculties so meek*
    Has exercised his authority so
    compassionately

8   *Striding the blast*
    Bestriding the wind

9   *I have no spur / To prick the sides of my*
    intent, but only / Vaulting ambition, which
    o'erleaps itself / And falls on th' other.
    The complex image comes from
    horsemanship. Macbeth claims he
    has no *spur* **to motivate him other**
    than *ambition* **itself, which threatens**
    to "vault" him completely over the
    horse he seeks to mount. (See
    LONGER NOTE, **page 292.)**

Act 1, Scene 7

Hautboys. Torches. Enter a sewer and divers servants [1] *with dishes and service over the stage. Then enter* **Macbeth**.

Macbeth

If it were done when 'tis done, then 'twere well
It were done quickly. [2] If th' assassination
Could trammel up the consequence and catch

only   With his surcease success, [3] that but° this blow

i.e., on Earth   Might be the be-all and the end-all here,°   5

But here, upon this bank and shoal [4] of time,
We'd jump the life to come. [5] But in these cases

in that   We still have judgment here, that° we but teach

Bloody instructions, which, being taught, return

impartial   To plague th' inventor. [6] This even-handed° justice   10

Delivers   Commends° th' ingredients of our poisoned chalice

i.e., Duncan's   To our own lips. He's° here in double trust:

First, as I am his kinsman and his subject,
Strong both against the deed; then, as his host,
Who should against his murderer shut the door,   15
Not bear the knife myself. Besides, this Duncan
Hath borne his faculties so meek, [7] hath been

blameless   So clear° in his great office, that his virtues

Will plead like angels, trumpet-tongued, against

murder   The deep damnation of his taking-off;°

And pity, like a naked newborn babe,

angels   Striding the blast, [8] or Heaven's cherubim° horsed

invisible   Upon the sightless° couriers of the air,

Shall blow the horrid deed in every eye,

overwhelm   That tears shall drown° the wind. I have no spur   25

To prick the sides of my intent, but only
Vaulting ambition, which o'erleaps itself
And falls on th' other. [9]

91

1 *the ornament of life*
   I.e., the crown

2 *wait upon*
   Accompany (as if a servant to)

3 *cat i' th' adage*
   I.e., the proverbial cat that wanted
   fish but didn't want to get its feet wet

4 *I dare do all that may become a man. /*
   Who dares do more is none.
   Macbeth is ready to do anything
   that is appropriate or fitting for a
   man; those who go beyond this
   limit sacrifice their humanity,
   becoming bestial. In his *Oration on*
   the Dignity of Man (ca. 1486), the
   humanist Pico della Mirandola
   claimed that humans were placed
   above the animals and below the
   angels in the chain of being. For
   Pico, human dignity was a
   consequence of being "a creature
   of indeterminate nature." Blessed
   with free will, humans "have the
   power to degenerate into the
   lower forms of life" or "to be
   reborn into the higher forms,
   which are divine." Lady Macbeth in
   response offers a perverse version
   of humanist aspiration—to be
   truly human is "to be more than
   what you were."

Enter **Lady** [**Macbeth.**]

—How now! What news?

Lady Macbeth

finished eating He has almost supped.° Why have you left the chamber?

Macbeth

Hath he asked for me?

Lady Macbeth

Know you not he has? 30

Macbeth

We will proceed no further in this business.

won He hath honored me of late, and I have bought°

Golden opinions from all sorts of people,

i.e., should Which would° be worn now in their newest gloss,

Not cast aside so soon.

Lady Macbeth

Was the hope drunk 35

Wherein you dressed yourself? Hath it slept since?

sickly And wakes it now to look so green° and pale

At what it did so freely? From this time

regard Such I account° thy love. Art thou afeard

To be the same in thine own act and valor 40

As thou art in desire? Wouldst thou have that

Which thou esteem'st the ornament of life, [1]

And live a coward in thine own esteem,

Letting "I dare not" wait upon [2] "I would,"

Like the poor cat i' th' adage? [3]

Macbeth

Prithee, peace: 45

I dare do all that may become a man.

Who dares do more is none. [4]

1 *Nor time nor place / Did then adhere*

   Neither time nor place was appropriate to the deed (when you first told me of your plans)

2 *They have made themselves, and that their fitness now / Does unmake you.*

   I.e., the time and place (for the murder of Duncan) are now ready, and now that they are both appropriate, that fact undoes you.

3 *screw your courage to the sticking-place*

   I.e., rouse your courage to its utmost limit. The image is of a crossbow, its string pulled fully taut.

4 *and the receipt of reason / A limbeck only*

   And the container of their reason (i.e., the brain) will become merely an alembic (the top part of a still, used to contain vapors in order to direct them for condensation)

Lady Macbeth

                What beast was 't, then,

divulge; broach   That made you break° this enterprise to me?

dared   When you durst° do it, then you were a man;

    And to be more than what you were, you would   50

    Be so much more the man. Nor time nor place

i.e., both advantageous   Did then adhere, [1] and yet you would make both.°

    They have made themselves, and that their fitness now

    Does unmake you. [2] I have given suck and know

    How tender 'tis to love the babe that milks me.   55

    I would, while it was smiling in my face,

    Have plucked my nipple from his boneless gums

    And dashed the brains out, had I so sworn as you

    Have done to this.

Macbeth

            If we should fail?

Lady Macbeth

            We fail?

Only   But° screw your courage to the sticking-place, [3]   60

    And we'll not fail. When Duncan is asleep—

    Whereto the rather shall his day's hard journey

chamber servants   Soundly invite him—his two chamberlains°

liquor / overpower   Will I with wine and wassail° so convince°

guardian   That memory, the warder° of the brain,   65

vapor   Shall be a fume,° and the receipt of reason

pig-like   A limbeck only. [4] When in swinish° sleep

drunken   Their drenchèd° natures lies as in a death,

    What cannot you and I perform upon

    Th' unguarded Duncan? What not put upon   70

drunken   His spongy° officers, who shall bear the guilt

murder   Of our great quell?°

1   *mettle*

Spirit or temperament (with a pun
on "metal" used to make "mail,"
or armor)

2   *I am settled and bend up / Each corporal*

agent to this terrible feat.

I have decided, and make ready
every muscle and sinew to
accomplish the murder.

Macbeth

                   Bring forth men-children only,
For thy undaunted mettle[1] should compose

understood   Nothing but males. Will it not be received,°
When we have marked with blood those sleepy two   75

own   Of his own chamber and used their very° daggers,
That they have done 't?

Lady Macbeth

otherwise   Who dares receive it other,°
As we shall make our griefs and clamor roar
Upon his death?

Macbeth

               I am settled and bend up
Each corporal agent to this terrible feat.[2]   80

deceive   Away, and mock° the time with fairest show;
False face must hide what the false heart doth know.

                            They exit.

1   *How goes the night*
    What time is it?

2   *that*
    **Presumably, Banquo has handed
    Fleance something else to hold,
    perhaps a piece of armor or his
    dagger.**

3   *Merciful powers, / Restrain in me the
    cursèd thoughts that nature / Gives way
    to in repose.*
    **Angels protect me from the evil
    thoughts that arise when at rest.
    (*Nature* is used here to mean
    "human nature" or "natural
    disposition.")**

4   *largess to your offices*
    Gifts to your household officers

5   *shut up*
    **Probably means "went to bed"
    (shut up in a chamber), but could
    mean "concluded his speech."**

Act 2, Scene 1

Enter **Banquo** *and* **Fleance** *with a torch before him.*

(Thane) (his son)

Banquo *(Thane)*
How goes the night,[1] boy?

Fleance *(Banquo's son)*
The moon is down. I have not heard the clock.

Banquo *(Thane)*
And she goes down at twelve.

Fleance *(son)*

                   I take 't 'tis later, sir.

Banquo *(Thane)*

thrift   Hold, take my sword. There's husbandry° in heaven;
            Their candles are all out. Take thee that[2] too.   5
i.e., need to sleep A heavy summons° lies like lead upon me,
            And yet I would not sleep. Merciful powers,
            Restrain in me the cursèd thoughts that nature
            Gives way to in repose.[3]

Enter **Macbeth** *and a* **Servant** *with a torch.*

                   Give me my sword.
            Who's there?   10

Macbeth
            A friend.

Banquo *(Thane)*
            What, sir? Not yet at rest? The King's a-bed.
good spirits   He hath been in unusual pleasure° and
            Sent forth great largess to your offices.[4]
with   This diamond he greets your wife withal,°   15
            By the name of "most kind hostess," and shut up[5]
            In measureless content. [*hands him a jewel*]

1   *Being unprepared, / Our will became the*
     servant to defect, / Which else should
     free have wrought.

     **I.e., our wish to entertain Duncan was
     hindered by our unpreparedness,
     which otherwise lavishly would have
     greeted him.**

2   *If you shall cleave to my consent, when 'tis*
     **If you will give me your support
     when the time comes**

3   *So I lose none / In seeking to augment it,*
     but still keep / My bosom franchised and
     allegiance clear, / I shall be counselled.

     **If I don't risk losing honor in
     seeking to gain more, but instead
     stay pure in my heart and
     untainted in my allegiance, I will
     listen to what you have to say.**

4   *Good repose the while!*

     Rest easily in the meantime!

Macbeth

Being unprepared,

desire / our deficiencies   Our will° became the servant to defect,°

freely   Which else should free° have wrought. [1]

Banquo (Thane)

All's well.

I dreamt last night of the three weird sisters.   20

To you they have showed some truth.

Macbeth

I think not of them.

find   Yet, when we can entreat° an hour to serve,

We would spend it in some words upon that business,

If you would grant the time.

Banquo (Thane)

At your kind'st leisure.

Macbeth

If you shall cleave to my consent, when 'tis, [2]   25

It shall make honor for you.

Banquo (Thane)

So I lose none

In seeking to augment it, but still keep

free (from guilt)   My bosom franchised° and allegiance clear,

I shall be counselled. [3]

Macbeth

Good repose the while! [4]

Banquo (Thane)

Thanks, sir. The like to you!   30

Banquo [and **Fleance**] *exit.*

1   *Is this a dagger which I see before me, /*
    The handle toward my hand?
    The dagger that Macbeth sees is
    not visible to the audience, and it
    is unclear whether the *fatal vision*
    (i.e., concerning matters of death
    or proceeding from fate) is a
    psychological hallucination or a
    supernatural phantasm. Macbeth
    concludes that his preoccupation
    with the murder (*the bloody business*)
    has caused him to see things that
    are not real. (See LONGER NOTE on
    page 292).

2   *fatal*
    Used throughout the play with a
    double sense, both "deadly" and
    "produced by fate."

3   *on thy blade and dudgeon gouts of blood*
    On your blade and handle splashes
    of blood

4   *informs / Thus to mine eyes*
    Creates these forms for my eyes

5   *half-world*
    I.e., the hemisphere in which it is
    night

6   *Witchcraft celebrates / Pale Hecate's*
    off'rings
    Witches make sacrificial offerings
    to *Hecate* (pronounced with two
    syllables, *Heck-it*), the goddess of
    sorcery. Hecate was associated
    with the Greek goddess Artemis
    (the Roman Diana) and her cult of
    the moon; hence, here she is *pale.*

7   *Tarquin's ravishing strides*
    Sextus Tarquinius was a Roman
    prince who raped Lucrece; Lucrece
    committed suicide, and her relatives
    led the rebellion that established
    the Roman republic (509 B.C.)
    Shakespeare made this legend the
    subject of his long poem *The Rape of*
    Lucrece (1594).

Macbeth

[to **Servant**] Go bid thy mistress, when my drink is
    ready,
She strike upon the bell. Get thee to bed.

                             [**Servant**] *exits.*

Is this a dagger which I see before me,

grasp   The handle toward my hand?[1] Come, let me clutch° thee.

I have thee not, and yet I see thee still.   35

perceptible   Art thou not, fatal[2] vision, sensible°

merely   To feeling as to sight? Or art thou but°

A dagger of the mind, a false creation,

fevered   Proceeding from the heat-oppressèd° brain?

still   I see thee yet° in form as palpable   40

As this which now I draw. [*He pulls out his dagger.*]

guide   Thou marshall'st° me the way that I was going,

And such an instrument I was to use.

Mine eyes are made the fools o' th' other senses,

Or else worth all the rest. I see thee still,   45

And on thy blade and dudgeon gouts of blood,[3]

Which was not so before. There's no such thing.

It is the bloody business which informs

Thus to mine eyes.[4] Now o'er the one half-world[5]

deceive   Nature seems dead, and wicked dreams abuse°   50

The curtained sleep. Witchcraft celebrates

Pale Hecate's off'rings,[6] and withered murder,

warned   Alarumed° by his sentinel, the wolf,

watchword   Whose howl's his watch,° thus with his stealthy pace,

With Tarquin's ravishing strides,[7] towards his design   55

1   *Thou sure and firm-set earth, / Hear not*
    my steps which way they walk, for fear /
    Thy very stones prate of my whereabout, /
    And take the present horror from the
    time, / Which now suits with it.

    You fixed and stable earth, don't
    listen to my steps or note which
    way they walk, lest the stones
    gossip about my movements (i.e.,
    by echoing), and with their noise
    break the ominous silence that is
    appropriate to the situation.

2   *Words to the heat of deeds too cold*
    breath gives.

    I.e., words alone will not get the
    job done.

3   *I go, and it is done.*

    Revealingly, Macbeth skips over
    the contemplation of the murder
    itself.

4   *The bell invites me.*

    Although Macbeth literally refers to
    the bell which he has asked his wife to
    ring (lines 2.1.31–32), he invokes the
    practice of ringing the church bell
    when someone dies. "The passing
    bell" is the subject of John Donne's
    Meditation 17, in his *Devotions Upon
    Emergent Occasions* (1624), which
    admonishes its readers: "No man is
    an island, entire of itself; every man is
    a piece of the continent, a part of the
    main. If a clod be washed away by the
    sea Europe is the less, as well as if a
    promontory were, as well as if a
    manor of thy friend's or of thine own
    were: any man's death diminishes
    me, because I am involved in
    mankind, and therefore never send
    to know for whom the bell tolls; it
    tolls for thee." Despite the
    opposition of severe Protestants,
    the tolling of bells in early modern
    England remained a powerful
    reminder of both community and
    sacred time. Compare to Ross's lines
    in Act Four, scene three: *The dead
    man's knell / Is there scarce asked for
    who* (4.3.170–171).

fixed; steady   Moves like a ghost. Thou sure° and firm-set earth,

Hear not my steps which way they walk, for fear

speak   Thy very stones prate° of my whereabout,

And take the present horror from the time,

bluster; threaten   Which now suits with it. [1] Whiles I threat,° he lives.   60

Words to the heat of deeds too cold breath gives. [2]

A bell rings.

I go, and it is done. [3] The bell invites me. [4]

Hear it not, Duncan, for it is a knell

That summons thee to Heaven or to Hell.   *He exits.*

1   *owl*

The owl's cry was often thought to portend death.

2   *fatal bellman / Which gives the stern'st good-night*

Lady Macbeth compares the owl to a night watchman who tolls the bell marking the hours, but also announcing an execution (so the bell can therefore be said to bid the most final good-night).

3   *possets*

Hot milk spiked with liquor, sugar, and spices.

4   Enter **Macbeth**

The Folio indicates Macbeth's entrance after line 2.2.13, which is not impossible, but which makes Lady Macbeth's unawareness of her husband's presence potentially awkward on stage.

5   *My husband!*

This is the only time in the play that Lady Macbeth refers to Macbeth as her *husband*.

Act 2, Scene 2

Enter **Lady [Macbeth**.]

Lady Macbeth

That which hath made them drunk hath made me
    bold.

What hath quenched them hath given me fire. [*a noise*]

Hark! Peace! It was the owl¹ that shrieked, the fatal
    bellman

Which gives the stern'st good-night. ² He is about it.

servants   The doors are open, and the surfeited grooms°   5

duty   Do mock their charge° with snores. I have drugged
    their possets³

So that   That° death and nature do contend about them

Whether they live or die.

Macbeth

                [*within*] Who's there? What, ho!

Lady Macbeth

Alack, I am afraid they have awaked,

And 'tis not done. Th' attempt and not the deed   10

undoes   Confounds° us. Hark! I laid their daggers ready;

i.e., Duncan   He could not miss 'em. Had he° not resembled

My father as he slept, I had done 't.

Enter **Macbeth** ⁴ [*with daggers*].

                     —My husband!⁵

Macbeth

I have done the deed. Didst thou not hear a noise?

Lady Macbeth

I heard the owl scream and the crickets cry.   15

Did not you speak?

1 *one did laugh . . . and one cried*

Probably these refer to Donalbain
and Malcolm, as does the *two* in
line 2.2.28.

2 *hangman's hands*

I.e., bloodied hands; the hangman
would often disembowel and
quarter the prisoner he had
hanged.

Macbeth

When?

Lady Macbeth

Now.

Macbeth

As I descended?

Lady Macbeth

Ay.   20

Macbeth

Hark! Who lies i' th' second chamber?

Lady Macbeth

Donalbain.

Macbeth

i.e., the bloody daggers   This° is a sorry sight.

Lady Macbeth

A foolish thought, to say a sorry sight.

Macbeth

There's one did laugh in 's sleep and one cried [1]

    "Murder,"   25

So that   That° they did wake each other. I stood and heard them,

themselves   But they did say their prayers and addressed them°

Again to sleep.

Lady Macbeth

        There are two lodged together.

Macbeth

One cried, "God bless us!" and "Amen" the other,

As if   As° they had seen me with these hangman's hands. [2]   30

Listening to   List'ning° their fear, I could not say "Amen"

When they did say "God bless us."

Lady Macbeth

Consider it not so deeply.

1   *After these ways*

   Of in this way

2   *Methought I heard a voice cry, "Sleep no
   more! / Macbeth does murder sleep"*

   **Because the Folio text does not use
   quotation marks to distinguish
   between direct and indirect
   speech, it is difficult to know for
   sure where the voice that Macbeth
   has heard stops and his own
   elaboration on the idea of sleep
   begins (see also 2.2.44–46). While
   one might be inclined to gloss over
   this problem on the grounds that
   it's all in Macbeth's head, this
   moment presents a parallel to the
   dagger scene and invites the
   audience to consider the
   possibility of agencies beyond
   Macbeth himself.**

3   *raveled sleave*

   **Unraveled (or, perhaps, tangled)
   thread. A *sleave* is a thin strand of
   silk obtained by separating a multiplied thread (though audiences
   inevitably hear "sleeve").**

4   *second course*

   **The main and most satisfying
   course of a meal; parallel to sleep
   after great exertion.**

5   *unbend*

   **Slacken (as opposed to *bend up* in
   1.7.79)**

Macbeth

why   But wherefore° could not I pronounce "Amen"?

I had most need of blessing, and "Amen"   35

Stuck in my throat.

Lady Macbeth

               These deeds must not be thought

If we do so After these ways.[1] So,° it will make us mad.

Macbeth

Methought I heard a voice cry, "Sleep no more!

Macbeth does murder sleep"[2]—the innocent sleep,

Sleep that knits up the raveled sleave[3] of care,   40

The death of each day's life, sore labor's bath,

Balm of hurt minds, great nature's second course,[4]

Chief nourisher in life's feast.

Lady Macbeth

                What do you mean?

Macbeth

Still it cried, "Sleep no more!" to all the house.

"Glamis hath murdered sleep, and therefore Cawdor   45

Shall sleep no more. Macbeth shall sleep no more."

Lady Macbeth

Who was it that thus cried? Why, worthy Thane,

You do unbend[5] your noble strength to think

So brainsickly of things. Go get some water

evidence And wash this filthy witness° from your hand.   50

Why did you bring these daggers from the place?

They must lie there. Go carry them and smear

The sleepy grooms with blood.

Macbeth

                I'll go no more.

I am afraid to think what I have done.

Look on 't again I dare not.

1   *a painted devil*

I.e., a painting of the devil

2   *gild*

Literally, to cover in gold leaf,
which was sometimes reddish.
Here Lady Macbeth uses the word
figuratively, with a pun on *gild/guilt*.

3   *Neptune's*

Belonging to Neptune, Roman god
of the sea

4   *Making the green one red*

The Folio punctuation (with a
comma after *one*) suggests that this
means "turning red the sea that
was formerly green" rather than, as
Samuel Johnson suggested,
"turning the green sea uniformly
red" (*one red*).

5   *Your constancy / Hath left you*
    unattended.

Your steadfastness has abandoned
you (i.e., you have lost your nerve).

Lady Macbeth

Weak   Infirm° of purpose!   55
Give me the daggers. The sleeping and the dead
Are but as pictures. 'Tis the eye of childhood
That fears a painted devil. ¹ If he do bleed,
with (the blood) I'll gild² the faces of the grooms withal,°
For it must seem their guilt.   *She exits.*
                                                          Knock within

Macbeth

                                      Whence is that knocking?   60
terrifies How is 't with me when every noise appalls° me?
What hands are here? Ha! They pluck out mine eyes.
Will all great Neptune's³ ocean wash this blood
Clean from my hand? No, this my hand will rather
turn bloody The multitudinous seas incarnadine,°   65
Making the green one red. ⁴

                    Enter **Lady** [**Macbeth.**]

Lady Macbeth

My hands are of your color, but I shame
i.e., cowardly To wear a heart so white.°   *Knock* [*within*]
                          I hear a knocking
At the south entry. Retire we to our chamber.
A little water clears us of this deed.   70
How easy is it then! Your constancy
Hath left you unattended. ⁵   *Knock* [*within*]

1   *occasion call us / And show us to be*
    watchers
    The situation (Duncan's murder)
    result in our being summoned
    (while still in our clothes), revealing
    that we have been awake all along.

2   *To know my deed, 'twere best not know*
    myself.
    I cannot simultaneously
    acknowledge the gravity of my
    action and still recognize myself as
    its author.

                       Hark! More knocking.

dressing gown   Get on your nightgown,° lest occasion call us

And show us to be watchers.¹ Be not lost

dispiritedly   So poorly° in your thoughts.   75

Macbeth

To know my deed, 'twere best not know myself.²

                       Knock [within]

Wake Duncan with thy knocking. I would thou couldst.

                       They exit.

1 Enter a **Porter**.

As he goes to open the gate to the castle, the drunken *porter* (gatekeeper) imagines the types of people he would be admitting if he were the porter at the gates of Hell.

2 *old turning the key*

I.e., he would have to open the gate frequently (implying that many newly damned souls would be knocking)

3 *Beelzebub*

A devil, referred to as "the chief of the devils" in Luke 11:15 and "the prince of devils" in Matthew 12:24.

4 *expectation of plenty*

In anticipation of high crop yields and therefore low prices.

5 *Come in time*

I.e., you've come just in time; Hell is ready for you.

6 *other devil's name*

The Porter is apparently too drunk to think of another devil's name.

7 *an equivocator*

Literally, one who uses words with double meanings with the intention of deceiving the listener; more generally, one who simply hedges, refusing to make a commitment. (For the historical background of this phrase, see LONGER NOTE, page 293.)

8 *could swear in both the scales against either scale*

Could swear to support either side of a legal case (an example of *equivocation*). The phrase is also an allusion to the *scales* of justice.

9 *who committed treason enough for God's sake*

Both "committed treason in sufficient degree to serve God well" and "committed terrible treasons, as is obvious" (*for God's sake*, here the common oath).

10 *for stealing out of a French hose*

I.e., being stingy with cloth. The *French hose* in question were worn in two different styles: long and wide legged (making it easy to steal cloth) and short and fitted (making it considerably more difficult).

11 *goose*

A pun on several figurative senses of *goose*, including (1) the tailor's iron; (2) venereal infection accompanied by swelling; (3) a prostitute; (4) as in the expression: "cook your goose" (i.e., undo yourself).

12 *the primrose way to the everlasting bonfire*

I.e., the pleasurable road that ultimately leads one to Hell.

13 *remember the porter*

I.e., tip the gate keeper. The phrase may also be directed at the audience itself: i.e., "remember the porter's comedic interlude as the play now resumes and continues on its tragic course."

Act 2, Scene 3

Enter a **Porter**. [1] *Knocking within.*

Porter *(@* macbeth's castle)

Here's a knocking indeed! If a man were porter of Hell-
gate, he should have old turning the key. [2] *(Knock [within])*
Knock, knock, knock! Who's there, i' th' name of Beelzebub? [3] Here's a farmer that hanged himself on th'

handkerchiefs expectation of plenty. [4] Come in time, [5] have napkins°   5

with enough about° you; here you'll sweat for 't. *(Knock [within])*
Knock, knock! Who's there, in th' other devil's name? [6]
Faith, here's an equivocator [7] that could swear in both
the scales against either scale, [8] who committed treason enough for God's sake, [9] yet could not equivocate   10
to Heaven. Oh, come in, equivocator. *(Knock [within])*
Knock, knock, knock! Who's there? Faith, here's an English
tailor come hither for stealing out of a French hose. [10]
Come in, tailor. Here you may roast your goose. [11]
(Knock [within]) Knock, knock! Never at quiet. What are   15
you? But this place is too cold for Hell. I'll devil-porter
it no further. I had thought to have let in some of all
professions that go the primrose way to the everlasting

Soon bonfire. [12] *(Knock [within])* Anon,° anon! I pray you,
remember the porter. [13] *[opens the gate]*   20

Enter **Macduff** *and* **Lennox**.
(Thane (Thane)
of
Fife)

1 *Marry*

Indeed. Deriving from the name of
Mary, mother of Jesus, the word
was used as a mild oath.

2 *stand to*

Not only in the military sense of
"stand at attention" (and then fall
asleep: *not stand to*), but also, have
an erection (but be unable to
maintain it).

3 *equivocates him in a sleep*

I.e., (1) makes him fall asleep; (2)
tricks him by fulfilling his sexual
desire only in a dream

4 *giving him the lie*

Many meanings of *lie* apply:
(1) accusing him of lying; (2) lying
to (i.e., deceiving) him; (3) causing
him to pass out; (4) covering him
with urine (urine used as detergent
was sometimes called *chamber-lye*).

5 *gave thee the lie*

Macduff plays along with the
Porter's punning: *gave thee the lie*
could here mean "called you a liar"
but also "laid you out flat."

6 *i' th' very throat on me*

To lie in the very throat = to tell an
outrageous lie, but the drink that
drove him to that lie was literally in
his *very thoat*.

7 *being too strong for him, though he took
up my legs sometime, yet I made a shift
to cast him*

I.e., the Porter wrestled with drink
and, though drink grabbed him by
the legs (i.e., made him stagger
drunkenly), the Porter was able to
throw drink down. *To cast* may also
mean "to vomit or give off the smell
of alcohol."

Macduff (Thane)

before   Was it so late, friend, ere° you went to bed,

That you do lie so late?

Porter

i.e., about 3 a.m.   'Faith, sir, we were carousing till the second cock,° and

drink, sir, is a great provoker of three things.

Macduff (Thane)

What three things does drink especially provoke?   25

Porter

turning the nose red   Marry, [1] sir, nose-painting,° sleep, and urine. Lechery,

sir, it provokes and unprovokes: it provokes the desire,

but it takes away the performance. Therefore, much

drink may be said to be an equivocator with lechery. It

makes him, and it mars him; it sets him on, and it takes   30

him off; it persuades him and disheartens him; makes

him stand to [2] and not stand to; in conclusion, equivo-

cates him in a sleep, [3] and, giving him the lie, [4] leaves

him.

Macduff (Thane)

I believe drink gave thee the lie [5] last night.   35

Porter

repaid   That it did, sir, i' th' very throat on me; [6] but I requited°

him for his lie, and, I think, being too strong for him,

though he took up my legs sometime, yet I made a shift

to cast him. [7]

1   Enter **Macbeth**

The Folio has Macbeth enter
before Macduff speaks, no doubt
reflecting the amount of time it
would take for the actor to arrive
down stage. Logically, however,
Macbeth must become visible to
Macduff only after Macduff asks
about him.

2   *slipped the hour*

I.e., allowed the appointed time to
slip by

3   *The labor we delight in physics pain.*

Work in which we take pleasure
makes the effort easy to bear.
(Here, *physics* means "alleviates.")

Macduff (Thane)

Is thy master stirring? 40

Enter **Macbeth**. [1]

Our knocking has awaked him. Here he comes. [**Porter** *exits.*]

Lennox (Thane)

Good morrow, noble sir.

Macbeth

Good morrow, both.

Macduff (Thane)

Is the King stirring, worthy Thane?

Macbeth

Not yet.

Macduff (Thane)

early He did command me to call timely° on him;

I have almost slipped the hour. [2]

Macbeth

I'll bring you to him. 45

Macduff (Thane)

I know this is a joyful trouble to you,

But yet 'tis one.

Macbeth

The labor we delight in physics pain. [3]

This is the door.

Macduff (Thane)

as to I'll make so bold to° call,

appointed For 'tis my limited° service. *He exits.* 50

1 *obscure bird*

The bird of darkness (i.e., the owl)

2 *The night has been unruly. . . . Some say*
the earth / Was feverous and did shake.

In the early modern period, belief in portents and prodigies (extraordinary events suggestive of a supernatural meaning) was ubiquitous. The fundamental assumption underlying this belief is that the various spheres of existence are connected so that a disruption in the human world is reflected by disruption in the world of nature or in the heavens. The question of what specifically causes a particular event, however, frequently remains obscure. In *Hamlet* (1.1.112–125), Horatio interprets the ghost as a portent and recalls the prodigies that preceded the assassination of Julius Caesar. Though belief in the significance of prodigies was widespread, their interpretation was, of course, subject to dispute. In Shakespeare's *Julius Caesar*, Cicero warns, "Indeed it is a strange-disposed time; / But men may construe things after their fashion, / Clean from the purpose of the things themselves" (1.3.33–35). In *King Lear*, Edmund voices outright skepticism about portents. Responding to his father's assertion that "These late eclipses in the sun and moon portend no good to us," Edmund comments: "This is the excellent

foppery of the world, that when we are sick in fortune, often the surfeits of our own behavior, we make guilty of our disasters the sun, the moon, and the stars" (1.2.104–105, 119–122).

3 *broke ope / The Lord's anointed temple and*
stole thence / The life o' the building

Macduff's description of Duncan as a temple that has been desecrated insists on his status as a sacred king, the *Lord's anointed*. The divine authority of kings was obsessively reiterated and refined under both the Tudor and Stuart monarchs; a frequently cited text in support of the doctrine was Romans 13.1–2: "Let every soul be subject unto the higher powers: for there is no power but of God, and the powers that be are ordained of God. Whosoever therefore resisteth the power, resisteth the ordinance of God: and they that resist shall receive to themselves judgment." Shakespeare's history plays subject this orthodox view to intense scrutiny. Cf. *Richard II*, "Not all the water in the rough rude sea / Can wash the balm off from an anointed king" (3.2.54–55). Though monarchy continues to matter in the major tragedies, it is never the central concern. In *Hamlet*, it is the confirmed regicide Claudius who opportunistically invokes the "divinity that doth hedge a king" (4.5.123).

Lennox (_Thane_)

from here   Goes the King hence° today?

Macbeth

plan to do   He does. He did appoint° so.

Lennox (_Thane_)

The night has been unruly. Where we lay,
Our chimneys were blown down and, as they say,
Lamentings heard i' th' air, strange screams of death,
And prophesying with accents terrible   55
disorder; commotion   Of dire combustion° and confused events
New hatched to th' woeful time. The obscure bird [1]
Clamored the livelong night. Some say the earth
feverish   Was feverous° and did shake. [2]

Macbeth

                                      'Twas a rough night.

Lennox (_Thane_)

memory   My young remembrance° cannot parallel   60
A fellow to it.

Enter **Macduff**. (_Thane_)

Macduff (_Thane_)

                              O horror, horror, horror!
understand; imagine   Tongue nor heart cannot conceive° nor name thee!

Macbeth _and_ **Lennox** (_Thanes_)

What's the matter?

Macduff (_Thane_)

Destruction   Confusion° now hath made his masterpiece.
open   Most sacrilegious murder hath broke ope°   65
The Lord's anointed temple and stole thence
The life o' th' building! [3]

Macbeth

                              What is 't you say? "The life"?

1 *gorgon*

   A female, snake-haired monster
   from Greek mythology whose face
   would turn anyone who looked on
   her to stone (Medusa is the most
   well known of the gorgons.)

2 *The great doom's image*

   Macduff compares the King's
   death to Doomsday, the
   apocalyptic day of God's final
   judgment.

3 *To countenance*

   (1) to behold; (2) to behave
   appropriately to

4 *Ring the bell.*

   It is possible that in the manuscript
   from which the play was originally
   printed this was an instruction for
   a sound effect rather than part of
   Macduff's speech (as it is printed in
   the Folio), and some editions,
   therefore, omit it from Macduff's
   speech.

5 *parley*

   A conference, often used for a
   battlefield discussion of truce.

Lennox (Thane)
Mean you his Majesty?
Macduff (Thane)
Approach the chamber and destroy your sight
With a new gorgon.¹ Do not bid me speak.   70
See and then speak yourselves.

                          Macbeth and **Lennox** *exit.*
                          Awake, awake!
Ring the alarum-bell. Murder and treason!
Banquo and Donalbain! Malcolm! Awake!

soft   Shake off this downy° sleep, death's counterfeit,
And look on death itself! Up, up, and see   75
The great doom's image!² Malcolm! Banquo!

spirits; ghosts   As from your graves rise up and walk like sprites°
To countenance³ this horror! Ring the bell.⁴

              Bell rings. Enter **Lady** [**Macbeth**].

Lady Macbeth

What's the business,
That such a hideous trumpet calls to parley⁵   80
The sleepers of the house? Speak, speak!
Macduff (Thane)
                                        O gentle lady,
'Tis not for you to hear what I can speak.

report   The repetition° in a woman's ear
Would murder as it fell.

              Enter **Banquo**. (Thane

1   *serious in mortality*

    Significant in life

2   *The wine of life is drawn, and the mere*
    lees / Is left this vault to brag of.

    The wine of life is drained, and all
    that's left for this wine cellar to
    boast of are the *lees*, or dregs.
    (Perhaps the entrance
    immediately following is a
    deliberate irony.)

3   *What is amiss?*

    Donalbain is asking what the
    matter is, but Macbeth responds
    (*You are*) that Donalbain himself is
    ***amiss* (deficient) because his father**
    has been killed.

O Banquo, Banquo,
Our royal master's murdered!

Lady Macbeth

Woe, alas!   85
What? In our house?

Banquo (Thane)

Too cruel anywhere.
Dear Duff, I prithee, contradict thyself
And say it is not so.

Enter **Macbeth**, **Lennox**, *and* **Ross**.

Macbeth

only / event   Had I but° died an hour before this chance,°
I had lived a blessèd time, for from this instant   90
There's nothing serious in mortality. [1]
trifles   All is but toys.° Renown and grace is dead.
The wine of life is drawn, and the mere lees
Is left this vault to brag of. [2]

Enter **Malcolm** *and* **Donalbain**. (King Duncan's
Sons)

Donalbain (Duncan's Son)

What is amiss? [3]

Macbeth

You are and do not know 't.   95
The spring, the head, the fountain of your blood
Is stopped. The very source of it is stopped.

Macduff (Thane)

Your royal father's murdered.

Malcolm (Duncan's Son)

Oh, by whom?

1   *pauser*
    I.e., that which should make us
    pause

2   *breach*
    A rift; a break in the walls of a castle
    or city under attack.

3   *Unmannerly breeched*
    Rudely clothed in blood. Dr.
    Johnson complained that this
    phrase and the various attempts to
    correct were "expressions not
    easily to be understood." However,
    his own proposed emendation—
    "Unmannly drench'd with gore"—
    has not often been adopted. The
    metaphor of *breeches* (trousers)
    gains resonance not only from the
    pun on *breach* (line 111) but also
    from the contemporary practice of
    breeching, a rite of passage in
    which a young boy gave up the
    long frock worn in childhood and
    put on breeches. For the aristocratic
    classes this transition also entitled
    the young man to carry a sword.
    Thus, here the diminutive daggers
    have been intiated in an
    unceremonious manner; at the
    same time, the metaphor connects
    manhood with the capacity to spill
    blood.

4   *Help me hence, ho!*
    Stage tradition holds that Lady
    Macbeth faints here; however, a
    controversy exists over whether
    this collapse is feigned in order to
    distract from Macbeth's weak
    justification for having murdered
    Duncan's grooms or is genuine.
    The question concerns her
    trajectory from determined plotter
    to diseased victim. The faint could
    be genuine; in which case, she
    would need to have recovered her
    equilibrium by the time of the
    banquet scene. Alternatively, a
    false faint would have her still very
    much in control.

5   *That most may claim this argument for ours*
    I.e., who have the greatest claim to
    discuss this subject (i.e., the death
    of Duncan)

Lennox *(Tnane)*

Those of his chamber, as it seemed, had done 't.

marked   Their hands and faces were all badged° with blood.   100

So were their daggers, which unwiped we found

Upon their pillows. They stared and were distracted.

No man's life was to be trusted with them.

Macbeth

Oh, yet I do repent me of my fury,

That I did kill them.

Macduff *(Thane of fife)*

Why   Wherefore° did you so?   105

Macbeth

Who can be wise, amazed, temp'rate and furious,

Loyal and neutral, in a moment? No man.

haste   Th' expedition° of my violent love

Outran   Outrun° the pauser, [1] reason. Here lay Duncan,

His silver skin laced with his golden blood,   110

And his gashed stabs looked like a breach [2] in nature

destructive   For ruin's wasteful° entrance; there, the murderers,

Steeped in the colors of their trade, their daggers

Unmannerly breeched [3] with gore. Who could refrain,

That had a heart to love, and in that heart   115

his   Courage to make 's° love known?

Lady Macbeth

                          Help me hence, ho! [4]

Macduff *(Thane)*

Look to the lady.

Malcolm *(Duncan's Sons)*

[*aside to* **Donalbain**] Why do we hold our tongues,

That most may claim this argument for ours? [5]

1   *here, where our fate, / Hid in an auger-*
    hole, may rush and seize us

    As the King's sons, Malcolm and
    Donalbain are now in danger.
    Donalbain describes their future
    (*fate*) as an enemy, hiding in a small
    hole (such as one made by an *auger*,
    or hand drill) and waiting to
    ambush them.

2   *Nor our strong sorrow upon the foot of*
    motion.

    Nor is our grief ready to be
    revealed or acted upon.

3   *our naked frailties hid*

    (1) dressed ourselves; (2) brought
    under control our shock and
    horror (though the phrase points
    at the poignant fraility of the
    human condition)

4   *and thence / Against the undivulged*
    pretense I fight / Of treasonous malice

    And from that position I will battle
    the yet unknown motives for this
    treason.

5   *manly readiness*

    (1) manly attire (i.e., clothing and
    weaponry for fighting); (2) manly
    emotions (i.e., resolute minds)

Donalbain (D's son)

[*aside to* **Malcolm**] What should be spoken here, where
 our fate,   120

Hid in an auger-hole, may rush and seize us?[1]

matured; ready Let's away. Our tears are not yet brewed.°

Malcolm (D'S son)

[*aside to* **Donalbain**] Nor our strong sorrow
 upon the foot of motion.[2]

Banquo (Thane)

Look to the lady.   [**Lady Macbeth** *exits, attended.*]

And when we have our naked frailties hid,[3]   125

That suffer in exposure, let us meet

discuss And question° this most bloody piece of work

doubts To know it further. Fears and scruples° shake us.

In the great hand of God I stand, and thence

motive; design Against the undivulged pretense° I fight   130

Of treasonous malice.[4]

Macduff (Thane)

                    And so do I.

All

                              So all.

Macbeth

quickly Let's briefly° put on manly readiness[5]

And meet i' th' hall together.

All

                         Well contented.

They exit [*leaving* **Malcolm** *and* **Donalbain**].

1   *The nea'er in blood, / The nearer bloody.*

This adage means, for Donalbain,
"the more closely related we are to
Duncan, the closer we are to being
murdered ourselves."

2   *There's warrant in that theft / Which*
    steals itself

I.e., at this time of danger, to steal
away is a justifiable form of theft.

Malcolm (D's son)

What will you do? Let's not consort with them.

task   To show an unfelt sorrow is an office°   135

easily   Which the false man does easy.° I'll to England.

Donalbain (D's sm)

To Ireland, I. Our separated fortune

Shall keep us both the safer. Where we are,

There's daggers in men's smiles. The nea'er in blood,

The nearer bloody. [1]

Malcolm (D's son)

arrow   This murderous shaft° that's shot   140

landed   Hath not yet lighted,° and our safest way

Is to avoid the aim. Therefore, to horse,

overly scrupulous   And let us not be dainty° of leave-taking

slip   But shift° away. There's warrant in that theft

Which steals itself [2] when there's no mercy left.   145

They exit.

1 *Threescore and ten*

Seventy years (the assigned length of human life in the Bible; see Psalm 90:10)

2 *this sore night / Hath trifled former knowings*

I.e., the terrors of this horrible night make everything I have seen before seem trivial.

3 *By th' clock 'tis day, / And yet dark night strangles the traveling lamp.*

According to the clock, it is day, and yet darkness stifles the sun.

4 *Is 't night's predominance or the day's shame / That darkness does the face of Earth entomb / When living light should kiss it?*

I.e., is it night's superior strength that makes it seem so dark when it should be light, or is day embarrassed to show itself? (See 2.3.52–53) The prodigies described here are not understood as predictive of harm to come but rather as reflective of the unnatural act of regicide. The examples of the owl killing the hawk and the horses attacking their keepers before eating each other involve inversions of the natural hierarchy: the owl is subordinate to the falcon as the horse is to its keeper. Ross and the Old Man believe that the murder of Duncan, an assault on hierarchy itself, has disordered nature.

5 *tow'ring in her pride of place*

Soaring at the apex of her flight

6 *mousing owl*

An owl that (normally) hunts mice on the ground.

7 *hawked at*

Attacked in the air

Act 2, Scene 4

*Enter **Ross** with an **Old Man**.*

Old Man

span
harsh

Threescore and ten[1] I can remember well,
Within the volume° of which time I have seen
Hours dreadful and things strange, but this sore° night
Hath trifled former knowings.[2]

Ross (Thane)

old man

               Ha, good father,°

i.e., the Earth

Thou see'st the heavens, as troubled with man's act,   5
Threatens his bloody stage.° By th' clock 'tis day,
And yet dark night strangles the traveling lamp.[3]
Is 't night's predominance or the day's shame
That darkness does the face of Earth entomb
When living light should kiss it?[4]

Old Man

                      'Tis unnatural,   10
Even like the deed that's done. On Tuesday last,
A falcon, tow'ring in her pride of place,[5]
Was by a mousing owl[6] hawked at[7] and killed.

Ross (Thane)

And Duncan's horses—a thing most strange and
    certain—

favorites

Beauteous and swift, the minions° of their race,   15
Turned wild in nature, broke their stalls, flung out,

as if

Contending 'gainst obedience, as° they would
Make war with mankind.

Old Man

ate (pronounced "et")

                  'Tis said they eat° each other.

Ross (Thane)

They did so, to th' amazement of mine eyes
That looked upon 't. Here comes the good Macduff.   20

1   *What good could they pretend?*

    **What plausible reason could they
    have alleged for committing the
    murder?**

2   *Scone*

    **Ancient city in Scotland (just north
    of modern Perth) where kings
    traditionally were crowned.**

3   *Colmekill*

    **Iona, an island in the Hebrides and
    the traditional burial ground of
    Scottish kings.**

Enter **Macduff**. (Thane of fife)

How goes the world, sir, now?
Macduff (T)

Why? See you not?
Ross T

Is 't known who did this more than bloody deed?
Macduff T

Those that Macbeth hath slain.
Ross T

Alas the day!
What good could they pretend?[1]
Macduff T

bribed
They were suborned.°
Malcolm and Donalbain, the King's two sons,   25
Are stol'n away and fled, which puts upon them
Suspicion of the deed.
Ross T

'Gainst nature still!
devour   Thriftless ambition, that will ravin° up
likely   Thine own lives' means! Then 'tis most like°
The sovereignty will fall upon Macbeth.   30
Macduff T

He is already named and gone to Scone[2]
crowned   To be invested.°
Ross T

Where is Duncan's body?
Macduff T

Carried to Colmekill,[3]
The sacred storehouse of his predecessors
And guardian of their bones.
Ross

Will you to Scone?   35

1   *Fife*

Macduff is Thane of Fife, ancestral
territory on the east coast of
Scotland, north of Edinburgh.

Macduff ⊤

No, cousin, I'll to Fife. ¹

Ross ⌐

i.e., to Scone   Well; I will thither.°

Macduff ⌐

Well; may you see things well done there. Adieu,

Lest our old robes sit easier than our new!

Ross ⊤

Farewell, father.

Old Man

blessing   God's benison° go with you and with those   40

That would make good of bad and friends of foes.

They all exit.

1   *It should not stand in thy posterity*

It (i.e., possession of the throne)
would not stay in your family line

2   *verities on thee made good*

Predictions they spoke about you
that have now become fact

3   *Why, by the verities on thee made good, /*
May they not be my oracles as well, / And
set me up in hope?

Banquo reveals himself to be
compromised. He suspects
Macbeth of murder, and yet his
own ambition keeps him silent.
(We see him struggle with "cursèd
thoughts " in lines 2.1.7–10).
Shakespeare's not-quite-innocent
Banquo is a far cry from the figure
described in Holinshed, where
Banquo is described as
encouraging Macbeth ("Banquo
jested with him and said: Now
Macbeth thou hast obtained those
things which the two former sisters
prophesied, there remaineth only
for thee to purchase that which the
third said should come to pass.")
and participating in the murder of
Duncan ("communicating his
purposed intent with his trusty
friends, amongst whom Banquo
was the chiefest, upon confidence
of their promised aid, he slew the
king"). The exoneration of
Banquo, King James I's ancestor, is
frequently explained as a judicious

compliment, but there is a deeper
logic at work. Shakespeare's
Macbeth is without *trusty friends*,
and the revision of Banquo's role
increases Macbeth's terrible
isolation. Furthermore, the
acknowledgment of confederates
might create the impression, an
impression that Holinshed
deliberately cultivates, that killing
kings in Scotland was business as
usual.

4   Sennet

Trumpet call

5   *we*

Macbeth has begun to use the "royal
we" (but note the ingratiating *I'll*
request in the next line).

6   *Command upon me*

I.e., command me as my king
(rather than *request*)

Act 3, Scene 1

Enter **Banquo**. T

Banquo T
Thou hast it now: king, Cawdor, Glamis, all,
As the weird women promised, and I fear
Thou played'st most foully for 't. Yet it was said
It should not stand in thy posterity,¹
But that myself should be the root and father   5
Of many kings. If there come truth from them—
are fulfilled   As upon thee, Macbeth, their speeches shine°—
Why, by the verities on thee made good,²
May they not be my oracles as well,
And set me up in hope?³ But hush, no more.   10

Sennet⁴ sounded. Enter **Macbeth** *as King,* Lady
[**Macbeth**], **Lennox**, **Ross**, *lords, and attendants.*

Macbeth
Here's our chief guest.
Lady Macbeth
              If he had been forgotten,
It had been as a gap in our great feast,
entirely   And all-thing° unbecoming.
Macbeth
formal   Tonight we⁵ hold a solemn° supper, sir,
And I'll request your presence.
Banquo T
              Let your Highness   15
i.e., your commands   Command upon me,⁶ to the which° my duties
Are with a most indissoluble tie
Forever knit.

1　*grave and prosperous*
　Wise and profitable

2　*Go not my horse the better, / I must*
　become a borrower of the night / For a
　dark hour or twain.
　I.e, unless my horse goes faster
　than I think it will, I will have to
　ride an hour or two into the night.

3　*bloody cousins*
　I.e., the murderous Malcolm and
　Donalbain

4　*cause of state / Craving us jointly*
　Affairs of state needing attention
　from both of us.

Macbeth

Ride you this afternoon?

Banquo

Ay, my good lord. 20

Macbeth

We should have else desired your good advice,

always Which still° hath been both grave and prosperous, [1]

In this day's council, but we'll take tomorrow.

Is 't far you ride?

Banquo

As far, my lord, as will fill up the time 25

now 'Twixt this° and supper. Go not my horse the better,

I must become a borrower of the night

For a dark hour or twain. [2]

Macbeth

               Fail not our feast.

Banquo

My lord, I will not.

Macbeth

lodged We hear our bloody cousins [3] are bestowed° 30

In England and in Ireland, not confessing

Their cruel parricide, filling their hearers

tales With strange invention.° But of that tomorrow,

besides that When therewithal° we shall have cause of state

Hurry Craving us jointly. [4] Hie° you to horse. Adieu, 35

Till you return at night. Goes Fleance with you?

Banquo

Ay, my good lord. Our time does call upon 's.

Macbeth

I wish your horses swift and sure of foot,

entrust And so I do commend° you to their backs.

Farewell.   **Banquo** *exits.* 40

1 *To make society / The sweeter welcome*
   To make (your) company more
   welcome

2 *Sirrah*
   Term of address for an inferior

3 *Attend those men / Our pleasure?*
   Are there men waiting for my
   summons?

4 *To be thus is nothing, / But to be safely*
   thus.
   It is nothing to be king unless I am
   safely so.

5 *in his royalty of nature / Reigns*
   I.e., in his natural, kingly quality
   there is

6 *dauntless temper*
   Intrepid quality

7 *genius*
   The attendant or guardian spirit
   that, according to classical Roman
   belief, accompanied an individual
   throughout his or her life (similar
   to the Christian concept of a
   guardian angel).

8 *Caesar*
   Octavius Caesar (Augustus);
   Shakespeare refers to the animosity
   between Mark Antony and Caesar's
   spirit in his *Antony and Cleopatra* (esp.
   at 2.3.19–22).

9 *an unlineal hand*
   I.e., the hand of one who is not
   descended from me

Let every man be master of his time

Till seven at night. To make society

The sweeter welcome, [1] we will keep ourself

Until   Till suppertime alone. While° then, God be with you!

                              Lords exit [leaving **Macbeth** *and a* **Servant**].

Sirrah, [2] a word with you. Attend those men   45

Our pleasure? [3]

Servant

outside   They are, my lord, without° the palace gate.

Macbeth

Bring them before us.   **Servant** *exits.*

                              To be thus is nothing,

of   But to be safely thus. [4] Our fears in° Banquo

Penetrate Stick° deep, and in his royalty of nature   50

should be Reigns [5] that which would° be feared. 'Tis much he dares,

in addition to And to° that dauntless temper [6] of his mind

He hath a wisdom that doth guide his valor

To act in safety. There is none but he

Whose being I do fear, and under him   55

My genius [7] is rebuked, as it is said

scolded; chided Mark Antony's was by Caesar. [8] He chid° the sisters

When first they put the name of king upon me

And bade them speak to him. Then, prophet-like,

They hailed him father to a line of kings.   60

without successors Upon my head they placed a fruitless° crown

And put a barren scepter in my grip,

by   Thence to be wrenched with° an unlineal hand, [9]

No son of mine succeeding. If 't be so,

defiled   For Banquo's issue have I filed° my mind;   65

1 *common enemy of man*

   The enemy of all men, i.e., the
   devil

2 *champion me*

   Fight against me; Macbeth is
   determined to resist fate's promise
   of a dynasty to Banquo's children.

3 *to th' utterance*

   I.e., to the death (from the French *à*
   l'outrance, meaning "to the greatest
   extremity")

4 *he*

   I.e., Banquo. Macbeth leads the
   two men to believe that Banquo is
   responsible for their misfortune.

5 *Passed in probation*

   Went over the evidence

6 *borne in hand*

   Deceived; misled

7 *instruments*

   Agents and/or legal channels

8 *To half a soul and to a notion crazed / Say*

   Suggest even to a half-wit or a
   demented mind

pious   For them the gracious° Duncan have I murdered,
bitter feelings   Put rancors° in the vessel of my peace
i.e., soul   Only for them, and mine eternal jewel°
           Given to the common enemy of man [1]
descendants To make them kings—the seeds° of Banquo kings!   70
jousting arena Rather than so, come fate into the list°
           And champion me [2] to th' utterance. [3] Who's there?

                     Enter **Servant** *and two* **Murderers**.

           Now go to the door and stay there till we call.
                                        Servant *exits*.
           Was it not yesterday we spoke together?
           First Murderer
           It was, so please your Highness.
           Macbeth
                                        Well then,   75
           Now have you considered of my speeches?
           Know that it was he, [4] in the times past,
           Which held you so under fortune,
           Which you thought had been our innocent self.
           This I made good to you in our last conference,   80
           Passed in probation [5] with you, how you
thwarted   Were borne in hand, [6] how crossed,° the instruments, [7]
worked   Who wrought° with them, and all things else that might
           To half a soul and to a notion crazed
           Say, [8] "Thus did Banquo."
           First Murderer
                                        You made it known to us.   85

1   *gospeled*
    I.e. virtuous, instructed by the
    teachings of the Gospels, which
    state: "Love your enemies and pray
    for those who persecute you"
    (Matthew 5:44)

2   *beggared yours*
    Made your family and descendants
    beggars

3   *in the catalogue ye go for men*
    In the general list (of species) you
    qualify as men.

4   *Shoughs, water-rugs, and demi-wolves*
    Shoughs (pronounced "shocks," as
    contemporary spellings suggest) are
    lapdogs; *water-rugs* are retrievers;
    demi-wolves are interbred animals,
    half-wolf, half-dog.

5   *valued file*
    List ordered according to the value
    of each item

6   *he does receive / Particular addition from
    the bill / That writes them all alike*
    Each species of dog is named and
    differentiated from the generic list
    that would see them all as "dogs"

7   *put that business in your bosoms*
    I.e., set you to that task

8   *execution takes your enemy off*
    Successful completion (execution)
    gets rid of (*takes . . . off*; i.e., kills)
    your enemy

9   *us, / Who wear our health but sickly in
    his life, / Which in his death were perfect*
    Me, who am sick while he (Banquo)
    lives, but would be perfectly
    healthy if he were dead

Macbeth

I did so, and went further, which is now
Our point of second meeting. Do you find
Your patience so predominant in your nature
That you can let this go? Are you so gospeled [1]
To pray for this good man and for his issue,   90
Whose heavy hand hath bowed you to the grave
And beggared yours [2] forever?

First Murderer

                                    We are men, my liege.

Macbeth

Ay, in the catalogue ye go for men, [3]
As hounds and greyhounds, mongrels, spaniels, curs,°
Shoughs, water-rugs, and demi-wolves [4] are clept°   95
All by the name of dogs. The valued file [5]
Distinguishes the swift, the slow, the subtle,
The housekeeper,° the hunter, every one
According to the gift which bounteous nature
Hath in him closed,° whereby he does receive   100
Particular addition from the bill
That writes them all alike. [6] And so of men.
Now, if you have a station° in the file
Not i' th' worst rank of manhood, say 't,
And I will put that business in your bosoms'   105
Whose execution takes your enemy off, [8]
Grapples° you to the heart and love of us,
Who wear our health but sickly in his life,
Which in his death were perfect. [9]

Second Murderer

                                    I am one, my liege,
Whom the vile blows and buffets of the world   110

mutts

called

watchdog

enclosed

position

Joins

1   *tugged with*
    Knocked around by

2   *in such bloody distance*
    In such dangerous enmity. As a
    technical term for the space
    between two fencers, *distance*
    draws upon the same fencing
    imagery as *thrusts* in the next line.

3   *near'st of life*
    I.e., my heart, the thing that most
    closely determines my life

4   *to your assistance do make love*
    Passionately solicit your help

angered   Hath so incensed° that I am reckless what
              I do to spite the world.
              First Murderer
                                 And I another,
              So weary with disasters, tugged with¹ fortune,
risk   That I would set° my life on any chance
of   To mend it or be rid on° 't.
              Macbeth
                                         Both of you   115
              Know Banquo was your enemy.
              Both Murderers
                                             True, my lord.
              Macbeth
              So is he mine, and in such bloody distance²
being alive That every minute of his being° thrusts
              Against my near'st of life.³ And though I could
              With barefaced power sweep him from my sight   120
justify   And bid my will avouch° it, yet I must not,
Because of For° certain friends that are both his and mine,
must grieve Whose loves I may not drop, but wail° his fall
              Who I myself struck down. And thence it is
              That I to your assistance do make love,⁴   125
              Masking the business from the common eye
              For sundry weighty reasons.
              Second Murderer
                                     We shall, my lord,
              Perform what you command us.
              First Murderer
                                         Though our lives—
              Macbeth
courage   Your spirits° shine through you. Within this hour at
                  most
              I will advise you where to plant yourselves,   130

1 *Acquaint you with the perfect spy o' th' time*

The meaning of this line is elusive, though it must mean something like "tell you the exact moment or place you should act."

2 *something from*

Some ways away from

3 *a clearness*

A clearance; i.e., freedom from suspicion

4 *rubs nor botches*

Rough spots nor flaws

5 *Resolve yourselves apart.*

Decide by yourselves, in private.

Acquaint you with the perfect spy o' th' time, [1]
The moment on 't, for 't must be done tonight,

keep in mind   And something from [2] the palace; always thought°
That I require a clearness. [3] And with him,
To leave no rubs nor botches [4] in the work,   135
Fleance, his son, that keeps him company,

important   Whose absence is no less material° to me
Than is his father's, must embrace the fate
Of that dark hour. Resolve yourselves apart. [5]
I'll come to you anon.

Murderers

                                    We are resolved, my lord.   140

Macbeth

straightaway   I'll call upon you straight.° Abide within.

                                    [**Murderers** *exit.*]

decided   It is concluded.° Banquo, thy soul's flight,
If it find Heaven, must find it out tonight.   [*He exits.*]

1   *doubtful*

    Tenuous; uncertain; anxious

2   *Using*

    (1) entertaining, keeping company with; (2) making habitual, getting used to

3   *Things without all remedy / Should be without regard.*

    I.e., we shouldn't worry about things that can't be fixed.

4   *poor malice*

    Incomplete or insufficiently violent (hence *poor*) plot

5   *Remains in danger of her former tooth*

    Is still at risk from her fangs, which are as dangerous as they were before (she was *scorched*)

6   *But let the frame of things disjoint, both the worlds suffer*

    If the structure of the universe is allowed to come apart, both Heaven and Earth will perish. (The line, unusually, has thirteen syllables, evidence perhaps of some error in transmission, or, perhaps, a metrical image of the very dissolution of order that is discussed).

Act 3, Scene 2

Enter [**Lady Macbeth**] *and a* **Servant**.

Lady Macbeth

Is Banquo gone from court?

Servant

Ay, madam, but returns again tonight.

Lady Macbeth

Say to the King I would attend his leisure
For a few words.

Servant

     Madam, I will.   *He exits.*

Lady Macbeth

     Naught's° had, all's spent,°   5
     Where our desire is got without content.°
     'Tis safer to be that which we destroy
     Than by destruction dwell in doubtful [1] joy.

Nothing is / used up

satisfaction

Enter **Macbeth**.

     How now, my lord! Why do you keep° alone,
     Of sorriest° fancies your companions making,   10
     Using [2] those thoughts which should indeed have died
     With them they think on? Things without all° remedy
     Should be without regard. [3] What's done is done.

stay

most wretched

any

Macbeth

     We have scorched° the snake, not killed it.
     She'll close° and be herself whilst our poor malice[4]   15
     Remains in danger of her former tooth. [5]
     But let the frame of things disjoint, both the worlds suffer, [6]

slashed

heal

1   *Malice domestic, foreign levy*

    Native (i.e., Scottish) malice,
    foreign armies (gathered against
    Scotland)

2   *gentle my lord*

    My gentle (i.e., noble) lord

3   *Present him eminence*

    Pay him respect

4   *unsafe the while that we / Must lave our*
    honors in these flattering streams

    For the moment vulnerable so that
    we have to wash (i.e., improve) our
    position by flattering others

5   *But in them nature's copy's not eterne.*

    Lady Macbeth may either mean
    (1) Banquo and Fleance will not live
    forever, since *nature's copy* (i.e.,
    their natural copyhold, or lease, on
    life) cannot be eternal; or (2)
    Banquo and Fleance will have no
    descendants (an individual child
    being a *copy* formed by *nature* in the
    parents' mold).

6   *black Hecate's*

    Black refers to Hecate's role as
    goddess of night (see 2.1.52,
    though note the different
    adjective; there she is *pale*, from
    her association with the moon).

Before	Ere° we will eat our meal in fear and sleep
	In the affliction of these terrible dreams
	That shake us nightly. Better be with the dead,
	Whom we, to gain our peace, have sent to peace,
torture rack	Than on the torture° of the mind to lie
delirium	In restless ecstasy.° Duncan is in his grave.
	After life's fitful fever he sleeps well.
neither	Treason has done his worst; nor° steel nor poison,
	Malice domestic, foreign levy, [1] nothing
	Can touch him further.

20

25

Lady Macbeth

Come on, gentle my lord, [2]

furrowed (i.e., frowning) Sleek o'er your rugged° looks. Be bright and jovial
Among your guests tonight.

Macbeth

So shall I, love,

And so, I pray, be you. Let your remembrance
Be applied Apply° to Banquo. Present him eminence [3]
Both with eye and tongue, unsafe the while that we
Must lave our honors in these flattering streams, [4]
masks And make our faces vizards° to our hearts,
Disguising what they are.

30

Lady Macbeth

You must leave this.

35

Macbeth

Oh, full of scorpions is my mind, dear wife!
Thou know'st that Banquo and his Fleance lives.

Lady Macbeth

But in them nature's copy's not eterne. [5]

Macbeth

There's comfort yet: they are assailable.
cheerful Then be thou jocund.° Ere the bat hath flown
secluded His cloistered° flight, ere to black Hecate's [6] summons

40

1 *shard-born*

Born in dung; (or, if the Folio's
spelling, "borne," is correct,
perhaps borne on wings that are
shaped like shards, or the wing
covers of an insect).

2 *rung night's yawning peal*

Announcing the onset of night
(with the hum of its wings)

3 *seeling*

Eye closing; the term refers to the
practice of sewing up the eyelids of
a hawk while training it.

4 *Scarf up*

Blindfold (an unusual use of *scarf* as
a verb)

5 *that great bond*

Though this phrase is often read as
referring to Banquo's tenure of life
(Cf. "bond of life" *Richard III* 4.4.77), it
needs to be understood expansively
to include the entire range of social
"bonds" that have a foundation in
nature (e.g. Cordelia's "I love your
majesty / According to my bond"
King Lear 1.1.92–93). Macbeth is here
implicitly rejecting the Aristotelian-
Thomist tradition, which maintains
that "a social instinct is implanted in
all men by nature" (*The Politics*). In the
same place, Aristotle observes: "he
who is unable to live in society, or
who has no need because he is
sufficient for himself, must be either
a beast or a god." What makes

Macbeth pale is not merely the
continuing existence of Banquo,
but the very fact of social solidarity
and obligation itself.

6 *rooky wood*

Forest where the rooks (crow-like
birds) nest

7 *hold thee still*

Remain steadfast

8 *Things bad begun make strong themselves
by ill.*

That crimes are made secure by
greater crimes was a proverbial idea,
with a distinctly literary pedigree.
"*Per scelera semper sceleribus tutum est
iter*," a line from Seneca's
Agamemnon, meaning, "the safe way
through crimes is always more
crimes," is quoted in *The Spanish
Tragedy* (3.13.6), a very popular
Elizabethan tragedy. Though
Macbeth takes the sentiment as a
reliable guide to conduct, its logic
insists that crime is ultimately self-
defeating.

The shard-born [1] beetle with his drowsy hums
Hath rung night's yawning peal, [2] there shall be done
A deed of dreadful note.

Lady Macbeth

                                   What's to be done?

Macbeth

chick (affectionate)   Be innocent of the knowledge, dearest chuck,°   45
                    Till thou applaud the deed. Come, seeling [3] night,
pitying   Scarf up [4] the tender eye of pitiful° day
                    And, with thy bloody and invisible hand,
                    Cancel and tear to pieces that great bond [5]
fearful   Which keeps me pale.° Light thickens,   50
                    And the crow makes wing to th' rooky wood. [6]
                    Good things of day begin to droop and drowse,
                    Whiles night's black agents to their preys do rouse.
                    Thou marvel'st at my words, but hold thee still. [7]
                    Things bad begun make strong themselves by ill. [8]   55
                    So, prithee, go with me.   *They exit.*

1   *But who did bid thee join with us?*

The identity of the Third Murderer
has occasioned a variety of
speculations (Ross, Macbeth
himself, or something abstract like
Destiny). Dr. Johnson identified
the perfect *spy o' th' time* (3.1.131) as
the Third Murderer. The likely
explanation is that Macbeth,
worried about the competence of
the first two murderers, has sent
them a supervisor, but this does
not entirely dispel the uncanny
quality of the scene.

2   *He*

I.e., the third murderer

3   *he delivers / Our offices and what we*
have to do / To the direction just

I.e., he told us of our responsibilities
down to the last detail

4   *within the note of expectation*

On the list of expected guests

5   *go about*

Are being walked around to cool
down

Act 3, Scene 3

Enter three **Murderers**.

First Murderer

But who did bid thee join with us? [1]

Third Murderer

                        Macbeth.

Second Murderer

He [2] needs not our mistrust, since he delivers
Our offices and what we have to do
To the direction just. [3]

First Murderer

                    Then stand with us.
The west yet glimmers with some streaks of day.   5
Now spurs the lated° traveler apace°
To gain° the timely° inn, and near approaches
The subject of our watch.

Third Murderer

                     Hark, I hear horses.

Banquo

[*within*] Give us a light there, ho!

Second Murderer

                      Then 'tis he. The rest
That are within the note of expectation [4]   10
Already are i' th' court.

First Murderer

                 His horses go about. [5]

Third Murderer

Almost a mile; but he does usually—
So all men do—from hence° to th' palace gate
Make it their walk.

Enter **Banquo** *and* **Fleance**, *with a torch.*

belated / swiftly

reach / convenient

i.e., where he dismounted

1   *the way*

    I.e., the best way to do it

Second Murderer
> A light, a light!

Third Murderer
> 'Tis he.

First Murderer

Stand to 't.   15

Banquo ⊤

It will be rain tonight.

First Murderer
> Let it come down.
> [*The* **Murderers** *attack* **Banquo**.]

Banquo ⊤

O treachery! Fly, good Fleance; fly, fly, fly!

Thou may 'st revenge —O slave!
> [**Banquo** *dies.* **Fleance** *exits.*]

Third Murderer

Who did strike out the light?

First Murderer
> Was 't not the way?[1]

Third Murderer

only There's but° one down. The son is fled.   20

Second Murderer

We have lost best half of our affair.

First Murderer

Well, let's away and say how much is done.   *They exit.*

1   *degrees*
    Social ranks (which determine
    their positions at the table)

2   *At first / And last*
    To one and all (or possibly "once
    and for all")

3   *state*
    Throne or chair of state

4   *encounter*
    Answer (perhaps by toasting her)

5   *Both sides are even.*
    Referring either to the balance of
    greetings between Lady Macbeth
    and her guests, or to the way the
    guests are evenly seated on both
    sides of the table.

Act 3, Scene 4

Banquet prepared. Enter **Macbeth**, **Lady [Macbeth]**, **Ross**, **Lennox**, **Lords**, *and attendants.*

Macbeth

You know your own degrees;[1] sit down. At first
And last,[2] the hearty welcome. [*The* **Lords** *sit.*]
Lords

                                Thanks to your Majesty.
Macbeth

the guests   Ourself will mingle with society°
And play the humble host.
i.e., the appropriate   Our hostess keeps her state,[3] but in best° time   5
request   We will require° her welcome.
Lady Macbeth

Pronounce it for me, sir, to all our friends,
For my heart speaks they are welcome.

Enter **First Murderer**.

Macbeth

See; they encounter[4] thee with their hearts' thanks.
Both sides are even.[5] Here I'll sit i' th' midst.   10
unrestrained/Soon/toast   Be large° in mirth. Anon° we'll drink a measure°
The table round. [*to* **First Murderer**] There's blood
    upon thy face.
First Murderer

'Tis Banquo's then.

1   *'Tis better thee without than he within.*
    It's better to see it (Banquo's
    blood) on you than have it remain
    in him.

2   *broad and general*
    Unrestricted and omnipresent

3   *The least a death to nature*
    The smallest (of which) was deadly

4   *Hath nature that in time will venom*
    breed; / No teeth for th' present
    I.e., has a quality that will, in time,
    develop into something
    dangerous; however, at the
    moment he presents no threat

5   *We'll hear ourselves*
    Confer with one another

6   *give the cheer*
    Entertain your guests (or, perhaps,
    offer a toast)

Macbeth

'Tis better thee without than he within. [1]

Is he dispatched?   15

First Murderer

My lord, his throat is cut. That I did for him.

Macbeth

Thou art the best o' th' cutthroats,

Yet he's good that did the like for Fleance.

paragon   If thou didst it, thou art the nonpareil.°

First Murderer

Most royal sir, Fleance is 'scaped.   20

Macbeth

[*aside*] Then comes my fit again. I had else been perfect,

immovable   Whole as the marble, founded° as the rock,

surrounding   As broad and general[2] as the casing° air;

cramped / pent up   But now I am cabined,° cribbed,° confined, bound in

annoying   To saucy° doubts and fears.—But Banquo's safe?   25

First Murderer

Ay, my good lord. Safe in a ditch he bides,

carved   With twenty trenchèd° gashes on his head,

The least a death to nature. [3]

Macbeth

Thanks for that.

young serpent   There the grown serpent lies. The worm° that's fled

Hath nature that in time will venom breed;   30

No teeth for th' present. [4] Get thee gone. Tomorrow

We'll hear ourselves [5] again.

[*The* **First**] **Murderer** *exits.*

Lady Macbeth

My royal lord,

You do not give the cheer. [6] The feast is sold

1   *The feast is sold / That is not often
    vouched, while 'tis a-making, / 'Tis given
    with welcome.*

    I.e., the meal that does not
    continually reassure its guests that
    they are welcome seems
    impersonal, like something
    purchased (at an inn).

2   *To feed were best at home; / From
    thence, the sauce to meat is ceremony. /
    Meeting were bare without it.*

    If one wants simply to eat, one
    does it best at home; when away
    from home, what makes eating
    worthwhile are the social rituals
    which give flavor to the event.
    Gathering together (with a pun on
    meeting/meat-ing) would be
    pointless without it.

3   *good digestion wait on appetite*

    I.e., enjoy what you are eating; *wait
    on* = attend, serve

4   *had we now our country's honor roofed*

    We would have all our country's
    nobility under one roof

5   *Who may I rather challenge for unkind-
    ness / Than pity for mischance*

    Whom I hope I will end up accusing
    of unkindness, rather than pitying
    him for some misfortune that has
    befallen him

6   *Lays blame upon his promise*

    Casts suspicion on the surety of his
    word

That is not often vouched, while 'tis a-making,

'Tis given with welcome. [1] To feed were best at home;   35

From thence, the sauce to meat is ceremony.

Meeting were bare without it. [2]

Macbeth

reminder   Sweet remembrancer!°

Now, good digestion wait on appetite, [3]

And health on both!

Lennox T

                                 May 't please your Highness sit.

Enter **Ghost of Banquo** *and sits in* **Macbeth**'*s place.*

Macbeth

Here had we now our country's honor roofed, [4]   40

dignified; gracious Were the graced° person of our Banquo present,

Who may I rather challenge for unkindness

Than pity for mischance. [5]

Ross T

                                 His absence, sir,

Lays blame upon his promise. [6] Please 't your Highness

To grace us with your royal company?   45

Macbeth

The table's full.

Lennox T

                        Here is a place reserved, sir.

Macbeth

Where? ___

Lennox T

Here, my good lord. What is 't that moves your

    Highness?

1   *upon a thought*

   In a moment

2   *air-drawn dagger*

   (Imagined) dagger existing in the air
   (*drawn* = [1] depicted; [2] carried by)

3   *Imposters to true fear*

   Mere counterfeits of real fear (since
   Macbeth has no actual cause to be
   afraid)

4   *Authorized by*

   Created by or, perhaps, vouched for

5   *but on a stool*

   I.e., on nothing except an empty seat

Macbeth

Which of you have done this?

Lords

What, my good lord?

Macbeth

[*to* **Ghost**] Thou canst not say I did it. Never shake   50
Thy gory locks at me.

Ross T

Gentlemen, rise. His Highness is not well.

Lady Macbeth

Sit, worthy friends. My lord is often thus

since   And hath been from° his youth. Pray you, keep seat.

The fit is momentary. Upon a thought[1]   55
He will again be well. If much you note him,

fit   You shall offend him and extend his passion.°
Feed and regard him not. [*aside to* **Macbeth**] Are you a
    man?

Macbeth

Ay, and a bold one, that dare look on that
Which might appall the devil.

Lady Macbeth

i.e., nonsense   Oh, proper stuff!°   60
This is the very painting of your fear.
This is the air-drawn dagger[2] which you said

outbursts / flinches   Led you to Duncan. Oh, these flaws° and starts,°
Imposters to true fear,[3] would well become
A woman's story at a winter's fire,   65

grandmother   Authorized by[4] her grandam.° Shame itself!
Why do you make such faces? When all's done,
You look but on a stool.[5]

Macbeth

Prithee, see there! Behold! Look! Lo! How say you?
[*to* **Ghost**] Why, what care I? If thou canst nod, speak too.   70

1   *charnel houses*

    A room or vault for storing human
    remains

2   *our monuments / Shall be the maws of kites*

    Our only *monuments* (graves;
    memorials) will be the *maws*
    (stomachs) of *kites* (scavenger birds)

3   *Fie*

    A reproachful exclamation

4   *Ere humane statute purged the gentle weal*

    Before the compassion of the law
    purified the commonwealth
    (making it *gentle*)

5   *twenty mortal murders on their crowns*

    Twenty fatal wounds on their heads

If charnel houses[1] and our graves must send
Those that we bury back, our monuments
Shall be the maws of kites.[2]   [*The* **Ghost** *exits.*]

Lady Macbeth

                                        What? Quite unmanned in folly?

Macbeth

If I stand here, I saw him.

Lady Macbeth

                                        Fie,[3] for shame!

Macbeth

Blood hath been shed ere now, i' th' olden time,   75
Ere humane statute purged the gentle weal.[4]
Ay, and since too, murders have been performed
Too terrible for the ear. The time has been
That, when the brains were out, the man would die,
And there an end. But now they rise again   80
With twenty mortal murders on their crowns[5]
And push us from our stools. This is more strange
Than such a murder is.

Lady Macbeth

                                        My worthy lord,
miss   Your noble friends do lack° you.

Macbeth

                                        I do forget.
wonder   —Do not muse° at me, my most worthy friends.   85
I have a strange infirmity, which is nothing
To those that know me. Come; love and health to all.
Then I'll sit down. Give me some wine. Fill full.

                    Enter **Ghost** [**of Banquo**].

1 *And all to all*

   I.e., and all good wishes to all men
   here

2 *Our duties and the pledge.*

   (We confirm) our loyalty to you and
   the toast you just proposed.

3 *Hyrcan tiger*

   Hyrcania was a country south of the
   Caspian Sea; its tigers were
   proverbially fierce (see Virgil's
   Aeneid 4.367).

4 *If trembling I inhabit then*

   I.e., if I tremble then

I drink to th' general joy o' th' whole table,

And to our dear friend Banquo, whom we miss.   90

are eager to drink   Would he were here! To all and him we thirst,°

And all to all. ¹

Lords

                 Our duties and the pledge. ² [*They drink.*]

Macbeth

Begone   [*seeing the* **Ghost**] Avaunt° and quit my sight! Let the

    earth hide thee.

Thy bones are marrowless, thy blood is cold.

sight   Thou hast no speculation° in those eyes   95

Which thou dost glare with!

Lady Macbeth

                 Think of this, good peers,

But as a thing of custom. 'Tis no other;

Only it spoils the pleasure of the time.

Macbeth

Any man might   [*to* **Ghost**] What man° dare, I dare.

Approach thou like the rugged Russian bear,   100

armored   The armed° rhinoceros, or th' Hyrcan tiger; ³

i.e., Banquo's   Take any shape but that,° and my firm nerves

Shall never tremble. Or be alive again,

a deserted place   And dare me to the desert° with thy sword;

call   If trembling I inhabit then, ⁴ protest° me   105

The baby of a girl. Hence, horrible shadow!

Unreal mockery, hence!   [**Ghost** *exits.*]

1   *special wonder*

    Particular notice or amazement

2   *You make me strange / Even to the*
    disposition that I owe

    You make me feel that I have not
    the courage I thought was mine
    (*owe* = own).

3   *Stand not upon the order of your going*

    I.e., do not delay by following
    protocols of rank in leaving

4   *Augurs and understood relations*

    Auguries (prophecies, usually
    those made by releasing birds and
    observing their flights) and the
    hidden connections in nature

Why so, being gone,
I am a man again. [*to the* **Lords**] Pray you sit still.

Lady Macbeth

You have displaced the mirth, broke the good meeting

wondered at With most admired° disorder.

Macbeth

i.e., ghosts   Can such things° be,   110

pass over And overcome° us like a summer's cloud,

Without our special wonder?¹ You make me strange

Even to the disposition that I owe,²

When now I think you can behold such sights

And keep the natural ruby of your cheeks,   115

When mine is blanched with fear.

Ross

                          What sights, my lord?

Lady Macbeth

I pray you, speak not. He grows worse and worse.

questioning Question° enrages him. At once, good night.

Stand not upon the order of your going,³

But go at once.

Lennox

                    Good night, and better health   120

Attend his Majesty!

Lady Macbeth

                    A kind good night to all!

                        Lords [and attendants] exit.

Macbeth

It will have blood, they say. Blood will have blood.

Stones have been known to move, and trees to speak.

Augurs and understood relations⁴ have,

1 *maggot-pies and choughs and rooks*
Three birds of the crow family
(*maggot-pies* = magpies; *choughs*,
pronounced "chuffs" = jackdaws),
which were used ritually by augurs
in order to make predictions

2 *secret'st man of blood*
Murderer most carefully hidden

3 *What is the night?*
I.e., what time is it?

4 *Almost at odds with morning, which is*
which.
I.e., almost dawn (the time of day
when *night* and *morning* are *at odds*
with one another, unable to be
clearly differentiated).

5 *How say'st thou that Macduff denies his*
person
I.e., what would you say if I told
you that Macduff refuses to come

6 *by the way*
Indirectly (via rumor or a spy's
report)

7 *should I wade no more*
Even if I were to wade no farther

8 *Which must be acted ere they may be*
scanned
Which (things) must be acted on
immediately, even before they can
be pondered at length

9 *the season*
May mean "the seasoning," i.e.,
something that preserves or gives
freshness to," but may also mean
"the period when something
happens"

10 *initiate fear that wants hard use*
Beginner's trepidation brought on
by a lack of experience

11 *yet but young in deed*
I.e., still novices in crime

By maggot-pies and choughs and rooks,[1] brought forth   125
The secret'st man of blood.[2] —What is the night?[3]

Lady Macbeth

Almost at odds with morning, which is which.[4]

Macbeth

How say'st thou that Macduff denies his person[5]
At our great bidding?

Lady Macbeth

                    Did you send to him, sir?

Macbeth

I hear it by the way,[6] but I will send.   130
There's not a one of them but in his house

paid to spy   I keep a servant fee'd.° I will tomorrow—
early   And betimes° I will—to the weird sisters.
determined   More shall they speak, for now I am bent° to know,
By the worst means, the worst. For mine own good,   135
other matters   All causes° shall give way. I am in blood
Stepped in so far that should I wade no more,[7]
would be / going   Returning were° as tedious as go° o'er.
will come   Strange things I have in head that will° to hand,
Which must be acted ere they may be scanned.[8]   140

Lady Macbeth

You lack the season[9] of all natures, sleep.

Macbeth

self-delusion   Come, we'll to sleep. My strange and self-abuse°
lacks   Is the initiate fear that wants° hard use.[10]
We are yet but young in deed.[11]   *They exit.*

1   *Act 3, Scene 5*

This scene is usually considered a non-Shakespearean addition perhaps by Thomas Middleton. (See "Editing *Macbeth*," page 295.)

2   *wayward*

Disobedient, perverse. (The designation is slightly ironic, since Macbeth's perversity here is his lack of loyalty to the witches.) The witches too are called *wayward*; see 1.3.32 and note.

3   *Acheron*

A river in Greek mythology's Underworld, traditionally the "river of woe"

4   *vessels*

Cauldrons and utensils for potions and spells

5   *I am for th' air.*

I will fly away.

6   *This night I'll spend / Unto a dismal and a fatal end.*

I.e., I will use tonight for a sinister and destructive purpose.

7   *a vap'rous drop profound*

A mist possessing transformative powers, which the moon was supposed to have dropped; *profound* may mean "heavy" and therefore ready to fall, or it may mean "of weighty significance."

8   *artificial sprites*

(1) deceitful spirits; (2) spirits created by artifice or skill (magic)

Act 3, Scene 5 [1]

Thunder. Enter the three **Witches**, *meeting* **Hecate**.

First Witch

angry   Why, how now, Hecate! You look angerly.°

Hecate

hags   Have I not reason, beldams° as you are,

Saucy and overbold? How did you dare

have dealings   To trade and traffic° with Macbeth

In riddles and affairs of death,   5

And I, the mistress of your charms,

secret   The close° contriver of all harms,

Was never called to bear my part

Or show the glory of our art?

And, which is worse, all you have done   10

Hath been but for a wayward [2] son,

Spiteful and wrathful, who, as others do,

Loves for his own ends, not for you.

But make amends now. Get you gone,

And at the pit of Acheron [3]   15

Meet me i' th' morning. Thither he

Will come to know his destiny.

Your vessels [4] and your spells provide,

Your charms and everything beside.

I am for th' air. [5] This night I'll spend   20

Unto a dismal and a fatal end. [6]

work   Great business° must be wrought ere noon.

Upon the corner of the moon

There hangs a vap'rous drop profound. [7]

I'll catch it ere it come to ground,   25

tricks   And that, distilled by magic sleights,°

Shall raise such artificial sprites [8]

As by the strength of their illusion

1   'Come away, come away,' etc.

I.e., a song about Hecate
beginning with these words
appears in Thomas Middleton's
play *The Witch* (3.3), and was fully
included in the 1673 edition of
Macbeth, a fact that has led some
scholars to conjecture that
Middleton wrote this scene. (The
full text of the song is printed in
the Appendix on pages 287–290.)

2   *in a foggy cloud*

Perhaps evidence that, at least in
indoor perfromances, machinery
disguised by stage fog lifted the
actor from the stage.

Shall draw him on to his confusion.

He shall spurn fate, scorn death, and bear   30

His hopes 'bove wisdom, grace, and fear.

over-confidence   And you all know, security°

Is mortals' chiefest enemy.

       Music and a song within: 'Come away, come away,' etc. ¹

Hark! I am called. My little spirit, see,

waits   Sits in a foggy cloud² and stays° for me.   [*She exits.*]   35

First Witch

Come, let's make haste. She'll soon be back again.

                             They exit.

1   *My former speeches have but hit your thoughts*

My previous words have merely coincided with your thoughts; i.e., I have only said what you've been thinking. (Lennox is being deliberately obscure in order to protect himself from the accusation of treason.)

2   *Which can interpret farther*

Which can follow things to their logical conclusion; i.e., you can fill in the rest.

3   *Only I say*

I will only say

4   *marry, he was dead*

The sense of the oath *marry* is "of course," or "but then again"; i.e., of course, Duncan was already dead when Macbeth pitied him (and he did not pity him before he was dead).

5   *Who cannot want the thought*

"Can want" would convey the sense directly: "who is able to lack the thought?" Here *cannot* combines with *want* to form a double negative that serves as an intensifier. This convoluted and indirect language is typical of the entire speech, which is marked by irony and innuendo. The language here is the opposite of the *broad words* that have led to the disgrace of Macduff.

6   *broad words*

incautious talk

7   *failed / His presence*

Did not appear

8   *due of birth*

Birthright (even though Malcolm is entitled to the throne by Duncan's designation, not by birthright—see 1.4.36–39 and notes)

9   *Of the most pious Edward*

By the pious Edward the Confessor (who reigned as king of England 1042–1066)

Act 3, Scene 6

Enter **Lennox** *and another* **Lord**.

Lennox T

My former speeches have but hit your thoughts, [1]
Which can interpret farther. [2] Only I say [3]

conducted　Things have been strangely borne.° The gracious Duncan

by　Was pitied of° Macbeth; marry, he was dead. [4]

And the right-valiant Banquo walked too late,　　　　5
Whom, you may say, if 't please you, Fleance killed,
For Fleance fled. Men must not walk too late.
Who cannot want the thought [5] how monstrous
It was for Malcolm and for Donalbain

deed　To kill their gracious father? Damnèd fact!°　　　　10

straightaway　How it did grieve Macbeth! Did he not straight°
In pious rage the two delinquents tear

captives　That were the slaves of drink and thralls° of sleep?
Was not that nobly done? Ay, and wisely too,
For 'twould have angered any heart alive　　　　15
To hear the men deny 't. So that I say
He has borne all things well, and I do think
That had he Duncan's sons under his key—

if　As, an° 't please heaven, he shall not—they should find
What 'twere to kill a father. So should Fleance.　　　　20
But peace, for from broad words, [6] and 'cause he failed
His presence [7] at the tyrant's feast, I hear
Macduff lives in disgrace. Sir, can you tell

lodges; keeps　Where he bestows° himself?

Lord

　　　　　　　　The son of Duncan—

withholds　From whom this tyrant holds° the due of birth [8]—　　　　25
Lives in the English court and is received
Of the most pious Edward [9] with such grace

1   *That the malevolence of fortune nothing /*   9   *suffering country / Under a hand*

    Takes from his high respect   *accursed*

    That his (Malcolm's) dire   **Country suffering under a**

    circumstances do not keep him   **detestable hand**

    from being received with proper

    courtesy

2   *upon his aid*

    On his (Malcolm's) behalf

3   *Northumberland and warlike Siward*

    The people of Northumberland

    (the English county bordering

    Scotland) and Siward, the Earl of

    Northumberland

4   *Free from our feasts and banquets bloody*

    knives

    I.e., have our feasts and banquets

    free from bloody knives

5   *Do faithful homage, and receive free honors*

    Offer heartfelt loyalty and receive

    honors as free men

6   *with*

    I.e., when Macduff responded with

7   *The cloudy messenger turns me his back /*

    And hums, as who should say

    (Macbeth's) sullen messenger turned

    his back and mumbled, as if to say

8   *Advise him to a caution, t' hold what*

    distance / His wisdom can provide

    I.e., caution Macduff to put as

    much distance between himself

    and Macbeth as he can manage.

That the malevolence of fortune nothing
Takes from his high respect. [1] Thither Macduff
Is gone to pray the holy King upon his aid [2]   30
To wake Northumberland and warlike Siward, [3]
That by the help of these—with Him above
To ratify the work—we may again
Give to our tables meat, sleep to our nights,
Free from our feasts and banquets bloody knives, [4]   35
Do faithful homage, and receive free honors [5]—
All which we pine for now. And this report
i.e., Macbeth   Hath so exasperate the King° that he
Prepares for some attempt of war.

Lennox T

Sent he to Macduff?   40

Lord

blunt; curt   He did, and with [6] an absolute° "Sir, not I,"
scowling   The cloudy° messenger turns me his back
And hums, as who should say, [7] "You'll rue the time
burdens   That clogs° me with this answer."

Lennox T

                  And that well might
i.e., Macduff   Advise him° to a caution, t' hold what distance   45
His wisdom can provide. [8] Some holy angel
relate   Fly to the court of England and unfold°
so that   His message ere he come, that° a swift blessing
May soon return to this our suffering country
Under a hand accursed. [9]   50

Lord

I'll send my prayers with him.   *They exit.*

1   *brinded*

Striped; multicolored; the cat is
probably the first witch's familiar,
Graymalkin (first mentioned in 1.1.8).

2   *Harpier*

The name of the third witch's
familiar or companion spirit

3   *Days and nights has thirty-one /*
Sweltered venom sleeping got

Has stored up venom secreted while
sleeping for thirty-one days and
nights

4   *fenny*

I.e., from a fen, or swamp

5   *blind-worm's sting*

The stinger of the *blind-worm* (a
small lizard)

Act 4, Scene 1

Thunder. Enter the three **Witches**.

First Witch

Thrice the brinded [1] cat hath mewed.

Second Witch

hedgehog Thrice, and once the hedge-pig° whined.

Third Witch

Harpier [2] cries, "'Tis time; 'tis time."

First Witch

Round about the cauldron go;

In the poisoned entrails throw.   5

Toad, that under cold stone

Days and nights has thirty-one

Sweltered venom sleeping got, [3]

Boil thou first i' th' charmèd pot.

All

Double, double toil and trouble,   10

Fire burn, and cauldron bubble.

Second Witch

Thin slice Fillet° of a fenny [4] snake

In the cauldron boil and bake.

Eye of newt and toe of frog,

Wool of bat and tongue of dog,   15

i.e., forked tongue Adder's fork° and blind-worm's sting, [5]

Lizard's leg and owlet's wing,

For a charm of powerful trouble,

Like a hell-broth boil and bubble.

All

Double, double toil and trouble,   20

Fire burn and cauldron bubble.

1 *maw and gulf*

Throat and stomach

2 *birth-strangled babe*

Dead baby strangled in delivery by the umbilical cord

3 *Ditch-delivered*

I.e., delivered in a ditch

4 *Round about the cauldron go; / In the poisoned entrails throw. . . . Cool it with a baboon's blood, / Then the charm is firm and good.*

No source has been identified for the witches' brew. Though it owes a debt to the notion of the witches' *sabbat*, a demonic feast at which witches were said to worship the devil, the catalogue of gruesome *ingredients* appears to be entirely Shakespeare's invention. Four elements, *Liver of blaspheming Jew, Nose of Turk, Tartar's lips,* and *birth-strangled babe*, point to recent changes in the laws concerning witchcraft under James I. In 1604 the Elizabethan statutes of 1563 were strengthened and extended. Among other things, the act of 1604 made it a capital offense to steal bodies or body parts for the purposes of witchcraft.

5 "Black spirits," etc.

The full song, like that after 3.5.33, was used in Middleton's *The Witch* and included in the 1673 Quarto edition of *Macbeth*. It is printed in the Appendix on pages 287–290. Many scholars believe that Middleton not only was responsible for the song but also for Hecate's lines in this scene.

Third Witch

Scale of dragon, tooth of wolf,

mummified flesh Witches' mummy,° maw and gulf¹

glutted Of the ravined° salt-sea shark,

Root of hemlock digged i' th' dark,   25

Liver of blaspheming Jew,

sprigs Gall of goat and slips° of yew

Cut Slivered° in the moon's eclipse,

Nose of Turk and Tartar's lips,

Finger of birth-strangled babe²   30

whore Ditch-delivered³ by a drab,°

sticky; viscous Make the gruel thick and slab;°

entrails Add thereto a tiger's chaudron,°

For th' ingredients of our cauldron.

All

Double, double toil and trouble,   35

Fire burn, and cauldron bubble.

Second Witch

Cool it with a baboon's blood,

Then the charm is firm and good.⁴

Enter **Hecate** *and the other three* **Witches**.

Hecate

efforts Oh, well done! I commend your pains,°

And every one shall share i' th' gains.   40

And now about the cauldron sing,

Like elves and fairies in a ring,

Enchanting all that you put in.

                    Music and a song: "Black spirits," etc. ⁵

                    [**Hecate** *and the other* **Witches** *exit.*]

1   *bladed corn*

Immature grain still tightly
encased in its husk (*corn* could be
used for any grain)

2   *Though palaces and pyramids do slope /*
Their heads to their foundations, though
the treasure / Of nature's germen tumble all
together, / Even till destruction sicken

An apocalyptic vision of complete
destruction—the principal image is
of a storm that flattens crops, trees,
castles, and palaces leading to the
ultimate destruction of *nature's*
germen (the seed, or material
essence, of all created things).
Compare "Crack nature's molds, all
germens spill at once / That make
ingrateful man!" *King Lear* 3.2.8–9;
"Let nature crush the sides o' th'
earth together / And mar the seeds
within." *Winter's Tale* 4.4.490. This
idea can be found in Augustine's *De*
Trinitate: "Some hidden seeds of all
things that are born corporeally and
visibly, are concealed in the
corporeal elements of this world. . . .
For the Creator of these invisible
seeds is the Creator of all things
himself; since whatever comes forth
to our sight by being born, receives
the first beginnings of its course
from hidden seeds, and takes the
successive increments of its proper
size from these as it were original
rules." The same idea may lie
behind Banquo's reference to *the*
seeds of time (1.3.58).

Second Witch

I can tell by / tingling   By° the pricking° of my thumbs,

Something wicked this way comes.   45

Open, locks,

Whoever knocks.

Enter **Macbeth**.

Macbeth

malignant   How now, you secret, black,° and midnight hags?

What is 't you do?

All

A deed without a name.

Macbeth

practice   I conjure you by that which you profess°—   50

Howe'er you come to know it—answer me.

Though you untie the winds and let them fight

foamy   Against the churches, though the yeasty° waves

Destroy / shipping   Confound° and swallow navigation° up,

flattened   Though bladed corn¹ be lodged° and trees blown down,   55

watchmen's   Though castles topple on their warders'° heads,

bend   Though palaces and pyramids do slope°

Their heads to their foundations, though the treasure

seed   Of nature's germen° tumble all together,

Even till destruction sicken,² answer me   60

To what I ask you.

First Witch

Speak.

Second Witch

Demand.

Third Witch

We'll answer.

1 *Thyself and office deftly show*
   Spoken to the apparition:
   "adroitly reveal yourself and your
   function"

2 an armed head
   A helmeted head

3 *harped*
   Touched upon, guessed (the word
   comes from finding the resonant
   string on a harp)

First Witch

thou Say if th'° hadst rather hear it from our mouths,
Or from our masters.

Macbeth

Call 'em; let me see 'em.

First Witch

Pour in sow's blood, that hath eaten
piglets / sweated out Her nine farrow.° Grease that's sweaten°   65
gallows From the murderers' gibbet° throw
Into the flame.

All

Come, high or low;
Thyself and office deftly show! ¹

Thunder. [Enter the] **First Apparition**, *an armed head.* ²

Macbeth

Tell me, thou unknown power—

First Witch

He knows thy thought.
nothing Hear his speech but say thou naught.°   70

First Apparition

Macbeth! Macbeth! Macbeth! Beware Macduff.
Beware the Thane of Fife. Dismiss me. Enough.

[The **First Apparition**]*descends.*

Macbeth

warning Whate'er thou art, for thy good caution,° thanks.
Thou hast harped³ my fear aright. But one word more—

First Witch

He will not be commanded. Here's another   75
More potent than the first.

1   *take a bond of fate*

    Bind fate with a contract (i.e., kill
    Macduff nonetheless). In this way,
    Macbeth can be assured of his
    safety both by Macduff's death and
    the apparition's prophecy.

2   *round / And top*

    I.e., crown (referring not only to
    the obvious shape and position of
    the crown but also to the fact that it
    rounds off, or completes, the
    desire for sovereignty and is the
    very *top* of secular ambition)

Thunder. [Enter the] **Second Apparition**, *a bloody child.*

Second Apparition
Macbeth! Macbeth! Macbeth!—
Macbeth
Had I three ears, I'd hear thee.
Second Apparition
Be bloody, bold, and resolute. Laugh to scorn
The power of man, for none of woman born   80
Shall harm Macbeth.

                                   [The **Second Apparition***] descends.*
Macbeth
Then live, Macduff. What need I fear of thee?
But yet I'll make assurance double sure
And take a bond of fate. [1] Thou shalt not live,
So that   That° I may tell pale-hearted fear it lies,   85
And sleep in spite of thunder.

                Thunder. [Enter the] **Third Apparition**, *a child*
                crowned, with a tree in his hand.

                                   What is this
offspring   That rises like the issue° of a king
And wears upon his baby-brow the round
And top [2] of sovereignty?
All
                       Listen, but speak not to 't.
Third Apparition
lion-hearted; brave   Be lion-mettled,° proud, and take no care   90
Who chafes, who frets, or where conspirers are.

1 *impress*

Order into (military) service

2 *Rebellious dead*

Sometimes, following Theobald, emended to "Rebellion's head" (i.e., army of the rebels), but *Rebellious dead* most likely refers to Banquo's ghost, which marks the metaphysical fear that haunts Macbeth.

3 *Macbeth / Shall live the lease of nature, pay his breath / To time and mortal custom*

I.e., Macbeth will live a natural lifespan (rather than suffer an untimely death). Here, Macbeth describes his mortal existence as something he *leases* from *nature*. The terms of that transaction require him to *pay* for his life with *his breath*. With the threat of murder eliminated, Macbeth can continue to pay his debts to *time and mortal custom* (old age and a natural death).

4 *noise*

I.e., the music of the hautboy, a wind instrument like the modern oboe

Macbeth shall never vanquished be until
Great Birnam Wood to high Dunsinane Hill
Shall come against him.

                        [*The* **Third Apparition**] *descends.*

Macbeth

                 That will never be.
Who can impress[1] the forest, bid the tree   95
omens   Unfix his earthbound root? Sweet bodements!° Good!
Rebellious dead,[2] rise never till the wood
Of Birnam rise, and our high-placed Macbeth
Shall live the lease of nature, pay his breath
To time and mortal custom.[3] Yet my heart   100
Throbs to know one thing. Tell me, if your art
Can tell so much: shall Banquo's issue ever
Reign in this kingdom?

All

                 Seek to know no more.

Macbeth

answered   I will be satisfied.° Deny me this,
And an eternal curse fall on you! Let me know.   105
Why sinks that cauldron? And what noise[4] is this?

                      Hautboys [*play.*]

First Witch
Show.
Second Witch
Show.
Third Witch
Show.

1 a show of eight kings

A procession depicting the eight
Stuart kings who ruled Scotland
from 1371 to 1625 (believed to be
Banquo's issue, or descendants). *The
last king, who walks with a glass in
his hand*, is James VI of Scotland.
James was crowned James I of
England in 1603 and was the
reigning monarch when
Shakespeare wrote *Macbeth*.
James's mother, Mary Queen of
Scots, is omitted from the
procession.

2 glass

Mirror

3 *th' crack of doom*

The *crack* that heralds the coming
of Judgment Day (possibly either a
thunderclap or the trumpeting of
an archangel)

4 *twofold balls and treble scepters*

Balls, or orbs, along with *scepters*
form a part of the regalia, the
distinctive ornaments of the
monarch that were used in
coronation ceremonies. Though
the precise application of the
terms has been disputed, it is likely
that the two balls were intended as
an allusion to the unification of
Scotland and England under James
I, while the three scepters allude to
rule over Great Britain, France, and
Ireland.

5 *blood-boltered*

I.e., blood-clotted or matted (hair)

6 *antic round*

Grotesque dance

All

Show his eyes and grieve his heart.   110

Come like shadows; so depart!

> [*Enter*] *a show of eight kings,* ¹ *and* **Banquo** *last;* [*the*
> *eighth king*] *with a glass* ² *in his hand*

Macbeth

Thou art too like the spirit of Banquo. Down!

Thy crown does sear mine eyeballs. And thy hair,

Thou other gold-bound brow, is like the first.

A third is like the former.—Filthy hags!   115

Pop out   Why do you show me this?—A fourth? Start,° eyes!

What? Will the line stretch out to th' crack of doom? ³

Another yet? A seventh? I'll see no more.

And yet the eighth appears, who bears a glass

Which shows me many more, and some I see   120

That twofold balls and treble scepters ⁴ carry.

Horrible sight! Now I see 'tis true,

For the blood-boltered ⁵ Banquo smiles upon me

as   And points at them for° his.   [*The vision vanishes.*]

What, is this so?

First Witch

Ay, sir, all this is so. But why   125

dumbfounded   Stands Macbeth thus amazedly?°

spirits   Come, sisters, cheer we up his sprites°

And show the best of our delights.

I'll charm the air to give a sound,

While you perform your antic round, ⁶   130

1   *Our duties did his welcome pay*
**Our performance was an
appropriate act of welcome.**

That this great King may kindly say
Our duties did his welcome pay. [1]

> *Music. The* **Witches** *dance and [then] vanish.*

Macbeth

Where are they? Gone? Let this pernicious hour

ever   Stand aye° accursèd in the calendar!
—Come in, without there.

> *Enter* **Lennox**.

Lennox

What's your Grace's will?   135

Macbeth

Saw you the weird sisters?

Lennox

No, my lord.

Macbeth

Came they not by you?

Lennox

No, indeed, my lord.

Macbeth

Infected be the air whereon they ride,
And damned all those that trust them! I did hear
The galloping of horse. Who was 't came by?   140

Lennox

'Tis two or three, my lord, that bring you word
Macduff is fled to England.

Macbeth

Fled to England?

Lennox

Ay, my good lord.

1   *The flighty purpose never is o'ertook /*
    Unless the deed go with it.

    **I.e., we never accomplish our
    fleeting intentions unless we act
    on them immediately.**

2   *That trace him in his line*

    That trace their ancestry to him

Macbeth

[*aside*] Time, thou anticipat'st my dread exploits.

The flighty purpose never is o'ertook   145

Unless the deed go with it. [1] From this moment

first impulses   The very firstlings° of my heart shall be

first (actions)   The firstlings° of my hand. And even now,

To crown my thoughts with acts, be it thought and
    done:

The castle of Macduff I will surprise,   150

Seize upon Fife, give to th' edge o' th' sword

His wife, his babes, and all unfortunate souls

That trace him in his line. [2] No boasting like a fool.

This deed I'll do before this purpose cool.

visions; hallucinations   But no more sights!°—Where are these gentlemen?   155

Come, bring me where they are.   *They exit.*

1   *When our actions do not, / Our fears do*
    make us traitors.

    I.e., even when we have not in fact
    committed treason, our fear (and
    consequent flight) makes us seem
    like traitors.

2   *He wants the natural touch*

    I.e., he lacks the natural instinct (to
    protect his *wife* and *babes*).

3   *All is the fear; and nothing is the love, /*
    As little is the wisdom, where the flight /
    So runs against all reason.

    He is motivated entirely by fear,
    and here is no sign of love, any
    more than there is wisdom, as his
    escape is so clearly unwise.

4   *coz*

    I.e., cousin, an affectionate form of
    address, not necessarily an
    assertion of kinship

5   *fits o' th' season*

    Strange behavior necessitated by
    these times

6   *when we are traitors / And do not know*
    ourselves

    When we are traitors without
    realizing it (because we are loyal to
    Scotland although not to the
    present king)

7   *when we hold rumor / From what we*
    fear, yet know not what we fear

    We believe rumors because we are
    afraid, but we do not know what we
    are afraid of.

Act 4, Scene 2

Enter [**Lady Macduff**], *her* **Son**, *and* **Ross**.

Lady Macduff

What had he done to make him fly the land?

Ross

You must have patience, madam.

Lady Macduff

                    He had none;

His flight was madness. When our actions do not,

Our fears do make us traitors. [1]

Ross

                    You know not

Whether it was his wisdom or his fear.   5

Lady Macduff

Wisdom? To leave his wife, to leave his babes,

His mansion, and his titles in a place

From whence himself does fly? He loves us not.

He wants the natural touch, [2] for the poor wren,

The most diminutive of birds, will fight,   10

Her young ones in her nest, against the owl.

All is the fear, and nothing is the love,

As little is the wisdom, where the flight

So runs against all reason. [3]

Ross

                 My dearest coz, [4]

control I pray you school° yourself. But for your husband,   15

He is noble, wise, judicious, and best knows

The fits o' th' season. [5] I dare not speak much further;

But cruel are the times when we are traitors

And do not know ourselves, [6] when we hold rumor

From what we fear, yet know not what we fear, [7]   20

And only But° float upon a wild and violent sea

1   *Each way and move*

A difficult phrase (often emended
to the no less obscure "each way
and none"); in either case it means
generally that, in these difficult
times, we are driven by events in
various directions rather than
choosing our course.

2   *It would be my disgrace and your*
    discomfort

I.e., I would break down and weep,
disgracing myself and making you
uncomfortable.

3   *Sirrah*

A term of address normally used to
social inferiors, but here used
affectionately.

4   *the net nor lime, / The pitfall nor the gin*

Methods for trapping birds; *lime* is
birdlime, a sticky paste applied to
twigs to catch small birds when
they alight; *the gin* is a snare.

5   *Poor birds they are not set for.*

People don't set traps for poor
(i.e., worthless; starving) birds.

Each way and move.[1] I take my leave of you;

It shall / before Shall° not be long but° I'll be here again.

Things at the worst will cease or else climb upward

To what they were before. [*to* **Son**] My pretty cousin,   25

Blessing upon you.

Lady Macduff

Fathered he is, and yet he's fatherless.

Ross

that should I am so much a fool, should° I stay longer

It would be my disgrace and your discomfort.[2]

I take my leave at once.   *He exits.*

Lady Macduff

                        Sirrah,[3] your father's dead.   30

And what will you do now? How will you live?

Son

As birds do, mother.

Lady Macduff

                What? With worms and flies?

Son

With what I get, I mean, and so do they.

Lady Macduff

Pitiful Poor° bird! Thou 'dst never fear the net nor lime,

The pitfall nor the gin.[4]   35

Son

Why should I, mother? Poor birds they are not set for.[5]

My father is not dead, for all your saying.

Lady Macduff

Yes, he is dead. How wilt thou do for a father?

Son

Nay, how will you do for a husband?

1   *With wit enough for thee*

**With surprising sophistication for
a boy**

2   *swears and lies*

**I.e., swears an oath of allegiance
and then breaks that oath**

3   *Was my father a traitor, mother? . . .
Then the liars and the swearers are fools,
for there are liars and swearers enough to
beat the honest men and hang up them.*

**Macduff's son provides a joking
and pathetic perspective on the
problem of defining treason that
animates this scene (see 4.2.4, 18,
and 81–82). His remarks point to
the connection between raw
power and the corruption of
language. A similar sentiment is
captured in Sir John Harrington's
epigram: "Treason doth never
prosper, what's the reason? / For if
it prosper, none dare call it
Treason."**

Lady Macduff

Why, I can buy me twenty at any market.   40

Son

Then you'll buy 'em to sell again.

Lady Macduff

Thou speak'st with all thy wit, and yet, i' faith,
With wit enough for thee. [1]

Son

Was my father a traitor, mother?

Lady Macduff

Ay, that he was.   45

Son

What is a traitor?

Lady Macduff

Why, one that swears and lies. [2]

Son

And be all traitors that do so?

Lady Macduff

Every one that does so is a traitor and must be hanged.

Son

And must they all be hanged that swear and lie?   50

Lady Macduff

Every one.

Son

Who must hang them?

Lady Macduff

Why, the honest men.

Son

Then the liars and swearers are fools, for there are liars
and swearers enough to beat the honest men and hang   55
up them. [3]

1   *in your state of honor I am perfect*
    **I am completely aware of your rank
    and reputation.**

2   *nearly*
    Quickly; imminently

3   *To fright you thus methinks I am too
    savage; / To do worse to you were fell
    cruelty, / Which is too nigh your person.*
    **I feel I am being cruel in
    frightening you this way; to do
    anything worse to you would be to
    act with savage cruelty—and
    cruelty of that sort is already close
    at hand.**

Lady Macduff

Now God help thee, poor monkey! But how wilt thou
do for a father?

Son

If he were dead, you'd weep for him. If you would not,
it were a good sign that I should quickly have a new   60
father.

Lady Macduff

Poor prattler, how thou talk'st!

*Enter a **Messenger**.*

Messenger

Bless you, fair dame! I am not to you known,
Though in your state of honor I am perfect. ¹

fear   I doubt° some danger does approach you nearly. ²   65

plain   If you will take a homely° man's advice,
Be not found here. Hence with your little ones.
To fright you thus methinks I am too savage;
To do worse to you were fell cruelty,
Which is too nigh your person. ³ Heaven preserve you!   70

stay   I dare abide° no longer.   *He exits.*

Lady Macduff

                              Whither should I fly?
I have done no harm. But I remember now
I am in this earthly world, where to do harm
Is often laudable, to do good sometime

Considered Accounted° dangerous folly. Why then, alas,   75
Do I put up that womanly defense,
To say I have done no harm?

1   *thou*

Lady Macduff's use of *thou* here
(like her son's in line 4.2.82) is a
dismissive use of the pronoun
taking force from its contrast to the
First Murderer's *your*. 17th-century
practice did not rigidly
differentiate the two second-
person pronominal forms, but in
contrast their use is often
expressive.

Enter **Murderers**.

What are these faces?

First Murderer

Where is your husband?

Lady Macduff

I hope in no place so unsanctified
Where such as thou¹ mayst find him.   80

First Murderer

He's a traitor.

Son

Thou liest, thou shag-haired villain!

First Murderer

infant   What, you egg?°

offspring   [*stabs him*] Young fry° of treachery!

Son

He has killed me, mother.
Run away, I pray you! [*He dies.*]

[**Lady Macduff**] *exits, crying "Murder!"*
[*followed by the* **Murderers** *with the body of her son*].

1   *Bestride our downfall'n birthdom*

Stand over our ravaged homeland
(to defend it as we would a fallen
soldier)

2   *Like syllable of dolor*

I.e., a similar cry of suffering (to
Scotland's)

3   *As I shall find the time to friend*

I.e., when I have the opportunity
(literally, "when I find that time has
become my friend")

4   *something / You may deserve of him*
    through me

I.e., you may gain something from
him by delivering me up to him. The
Folio prints "discerne," and it is
possible Malcolm means that
Macduff may discern in Malcolm a
future tyrant like Macbeth. The
emendation, however, makes more
sense with what follows and could
easily be misread in manuscript.

5   *A good and virtuous nature may recoil /*
    In an imperial charge.

A person's good and virtuous
nature sometimes gives way under
pressure from royal command.
Malcolm suggests that Macduff
might betray him to Macbeth.

6   *the brightest*

I.e., the brightest angel, Lucifer
(from Isaiah 14:12)

Act 4, Scene 3

Enter **Malcolm** *and* **Macduff**.

Malcolm (Duncan's son)

Let us seek out some desolate shade and there
Weep our sad bosoms empty.

Macduff (Thane of Fife)

                    Let us rather

deadly   Hold fast the mortal° sword and, like good men,
Bestride our downfall'n birthdom. [1] Each new morn
New widows howl, new orphans cry, new sorrows   5
so that   Strike Heaven on the face, that° it resounds
As if it felt with Scotland and yelled out
Like syllable of dolor. [2]

Malcolm (D's son)

              What I believe, I'll wail;
What know, believe; and what I can, redress,
As I shall find the time to friend, [3] I will.   10
What you have spoke, it may be so perchance.
mere   This tyrant, whose sole° name blisters our tongues,
honorable   Was once thought honest.° You have loved him well.
injured   He hath not touched° you yet. I am young, but something
it is wise   You may deserve of him through me, [4] and wisdom°   15
To offer up a weak, poor, innocent lamb
T' appease an angry god.

Macduff (Thane)

I am not treacherous.

Malcolm (D's son)

              But Macbeth is.
A good and virtuous nature may recoil
In an imperial charge. [5] But I shall crave your pardon.   20
change   That which you are, my thoughts cannot transpose.°
Angels are bright still, though the brightest [6] fell.

1   *Though all things foul would wear the*
    brows of grace, / Yet grace must still look so.
    Though evil things will pretend to
    be virtuous, the truly virtuous
    must nonetheless continue to look
    as they really are.

2   *my hopes*
    I.e., that you would return to
    reclaim Scotland from Macbeth

3   *Perchance even there*
    Perhaps in that same place (i.e.,
    mistrust)

4   *precious motives*
    I.e., beloved persons that should
    have inspired your protection of
    them

5   *Let not my jealousies be your dishonors, /*
    But mine own safeties
    Do not let my suspicions insult
    you; rather, they merely indicate
    my own caution to protect myself

6   *rightly just*
    Completely honorable

7   *Wear thou thy wrongs*
    I.e., continue to exercise your
    wrongfully gained power

8   *The title is affeered*
    Macbeth's claim to the throne is
    confirmed; but the inevitable pun
    on *affeered / afeared* also suggests
    that the (rightful) king, Malcolm, is
    afraid to challenge Macbeth.

9   *to boot*
    in addition, as well

10 *England*
    I.e., the King of England

Though all things foul would wear the brows of grace,
Yet grace must still look so. [1]
Macduff (Thane)

                       I have lost my hopes. [2]
Malcolm (D's son)

Perchance even there [3] where I did find my doubts.   25

vulnerable state   Why in that rawness° left you wife and child,

Those precious motives, [4] those strong knots of love,

Without leave-taking? I pray you,

suspicions   Let not my jealousies° be your dishonors,

But mine own safeties. [5] You may be rightly just, [6]   30

Whatever I shall think.

Macduff T

                  Bleed, bleed, poor country!

foundation   Great tyranny, lay thou thy basis° sure,

confront   For goodness dare not check° thee. Wear thou thy
       wrongs; [7]

The title is affeered. [8]—Fare thee well, lord.

I would not be the villain that thou think'st   35

For the whole space that's in the tyrant's grasp,

And the rich East to boot. [9]

Malcolm (D's son)

                 Be not offended.

distrust   I speak not as in absolute fear° of you.

I think our country sinks beneath the yoke;

It weeps, it bleeds, and each new day a gash   40

also   Is added to her wounds. I think withal°

There would be hands uplifted in my right,

And here from gracious England [10] have I offer

thousands (of troops)   Of goodly thousands.° But for all this,

When I shall tread upon the tyrant's head,   45

i.e., Macbeth's head   Or wear it° on my sword, yet my poor country

Shall have more vices than it had before,

1 *More suffer*

(Shall) suffer more

2 *and more sundry*

And (suffer in) more diverse

3 *voluptuousness*

Addiction to carnal indulgences

4 *Boundless intemperance / In nature is a*
tyranny.

I.e., unrestrained self-indulgence
represents a tyranny of the
appetites over a person's self.

5 *Convey your pleasures in a spacious*
plenty

Enjoy your desires in vast quanity
(*Convey* = carry on; conduct)

More suffer, [1] and more sundry [2] ways than ever,

By him that shall succeed.

Macduff T

Who   What° should he be?

Malcolm (D's son)

It is myself I mean, in whom I know   50

varieties / implanted   All the particulars° of vice so grafted°

displayed   That, when they shall be opened,° black Macbeth

Will seem as pure as snow, and the poor state

Esteem him as a lamb, being compared

boundless   With my confineless° harms.

Macduff T

                              Not in the legions   55

Of horrid Hell can come a devil more damned

In evils to top Macbeth.

Malcolm (D's son)

that he is   I grant him° bloody,

Lecherous   Luxurious,° avaricious, false, deceitful,

Violent   Sudden,° malicious, smacking of every sin

That has a name. But there's no bottom, none,   60

In my voluptuousness. [3] Your wives, your daughters,

Your matrons, and your maids could not fill up

tank   The cistern° of my lust, and my desire

self-restraining; chaste   All continent° impediments would o'erbear

desire   That did oppose my will.° Better Macbeth   65

Than such an one to reign.

Macduff T

                              Boundless intemperance

In nature is a tyranny. [4] It hath been

Th' untimely emptying of the happy throne

nevertheless   And fall of many kings. But fear not yet°

To take upon you what is yours. You may   70

Convey your pleasures in a spacious plenty [5]

1   *the time you may so hoodwink*

The age you may so mislead
(*hoodwink* literally means
"blindfold")

2   *my more-having would be as a sauce / To
make me hunger more*

I.e., the more I have, the more it
will make me want

3   *summer-seeming*

Summer-like (both hot and
transient), or perhaps, usual in the
summer of a man's life (i.e., in his
early adulthood)

4   *Of your mere own*

Out of your own royal estates

5   *king-becoming graces*

I.e., the qualities that mark (or
establish the excellence of) a king. In
Holinshed's account of this
exchange, Malcolm, having already
confessed to lustfulness and avarice,
reaches the limit of Macduff's
patience when he says that he
rejoices "in nothing so much, as to
betray & deceive such as put any trust
or confidence in my words. Then
since there is nothing that more
becommeth a prince than
constancy, verity, truth, and justice,
with the other laudable fellowship of
those fair and noble virtues which
are comprehended in soothfastness,
and that lying utterly ouerthroweth
the same; you see how unable I am
to govern any province or region."

Shakespeare's Malcolm does not
identify truthfulness (*soothfastness*)
as a comprehensive virtue that
includes the other *king-becoming
graces*; however, like Malcolm in
Holinshed's account, he pretends
to commit himself to the same
anti-social principle in his desire to
confound / All unity on Earth
(4.3.99–100), though, of course,
his lying here to test Macduff, is, he
says, his *first false speaking* (though
interestingly spoken more to
protect himself than, as in
Holinshed, to protect Scotland).

indifferent; chaste   And yet seem cold;° the time you may so hoodwink. ¹
                         We have willing dames enough. There cannot be
                         That vulture in you to devour so many
                         As will to greatness dedicate themselves,   75
i.e., greatness   Finding it° so inclined.
                         Malcolm (D's son)
                                                    With this there grows
disposition   In my most ill-composed affection° such
unquenchable   A stanchless° avarice that, were I king,
                         I should cut off the nobles for their lands,
                         Desire his jewels and this other's house,   80
                         And my more-having would be as a sauce
                         To make me hunger more, ² that I should forge
                         Quarrels unjust against the good and loyal,
                         Destroying them for wealth.
                         Macduff ⊤
                                                    This avarice
                         Sticks deeper, grows with more pernicious root   85
                         Than summer-seeming³ lust, and it hath been
i.e., downfall   The sword° of our slain kings. Yet do not fear;
abundance   Scotland hath foisons° to fill up your will,
these sins / bearable Of your mere own. ⁴ All these° are portable,°
balanced   With other graces weighed.°   90
                         Malcolm (D´s son)
                         But I have none. The king-becoming graces, ⁵
Such as   As° justice, verity, temp'rance, stableness,
humility   Bounty, perseverance, mercy, lowliness,°
                         Devotion, patience, courage, fortitude,
trace   I have no relish° of them but abound   95
variations / individual In the division° of each several° crime,
                         Acting it many ways. Nay, had I power, I should
                         Pour the sweet milk of concord into Hell,

1   *interdiction*

    I.e., prohibition (*Interdiction* is also
    a legal term, referring to the
    restraint of someone deemed
    unfit to act.)

2   *blaspheme his breed*

    Shame his family (by his behavior)

3   *Died*

    "Mortified herself" in religious
    exercise (i.e., did penance)

4   *modest wisdom plucks me*

    Prudent caution keeps me

Turn to chaos Uproar° the universal peace, confound

All unity on Earth.

Macduff T

                    O Scotland, Scotland! 100

Malcolm (D 's son)

If such a one be fit to govern, speak.

I am as I have spoken.

Macduff T

                    Fit to govern?

No, not to live.—O nation miserable,

illegitimate With an untitled° tyrant bloody-sceptered,

When shalt thou see thy wholesome days again, 105

most legitimate Since that the truest° issue of thy throne

By his own interdiction [1] stands accursed

And does blaspheme his breed? [2]—Thy royal father

Was a most sainted king. The Queen that bore thee,

(in prayer) Oft'ner upon her knees° than on her feet, 110

Died [3] every day she lived. Fare thee well!

These evils thou repeat'st upon thyself

Have banished me from Scotland.—O my breast,

Thy hope ends here!

Malcolm (D 's son)

                    Macduff, this noble passion,

Child of integrity, hath from my soul 115

doubts Wiped the black scruples,° reconciled my thoughts

To thy good truth and honor. Devilish Macbeth

tricks By many of these trains° hath sought to win me

Into his power, and modest wisdom plucks me [4]

From overcredulous haste. But God above 120

Deal between thee and me, for even now

I put myself to thy direction and

Retract / disavow Unspeak° mine own detraction, here abjure°

The taints and blames I laid upon myself

1 *Unknown to woman*
   I.e., with no sexual experience

2 *never was forsworn*
   Have never perjured myself or
   sworn falsely

3 *My first false speaking / Was this upon
   myself.*
   The first time I ever lied was just
   now, when I described myself as
   depraved.

4 *at a point*
   Fully prepared

5 *the chance of goodness / Be like our
   warranted quarrel*
   May the chance of our success be
   proportionate to the legitimacy of
   our cause

6 *convinces / The great assay of art*
   Overcomes the best attempts of
   medical skill

7 *but at his touch, / Such sanctity hath
   Heaven given his hand, / They
   presently amend*
   But Heaven has so sanctified his
   (Edward's) hand that his touch
   immediately heals them

_As_   For° strangers to my nature. I am yet   125
Unknown to woman,[1] never was forsworn,[2]
Scarcely have coveted what was mine own,
At no time broke my faith, would not betray
The devil to his fellow, and delight
No less in truth than life. My first false speaking   130
against   Was this upon° myself.[3] What I am truly,
Is thine and my poor country's to command.
i.e., arrival   Whither indeed, before thy here-approach,°
armed   Old Siward, with ten thousand warlike° men,
Already at a point,[4] was setting forth.   135
success   Now we'll together, and the chance of goodness°
justified   Be like our warranted° quarrel![5] Why are you silent?

Macduff
Such welcome and unwelcome things at once
'Tis hard to reconcile.

Enter a **Doctor.**

Malcolm (D's son)
Well, more anon.—Comes the King forth, I pray you?   140
Doctor
Ay, sir; there are a crew of wretched souls
await   That stay° his cure. Their malady convinces
The great assay of art,[6] but at his touch,
Such sanctity hath Heaven given his hand,
They presently amend.[7]
Malcolm (D's son)
                I thank you, doctor.   145
                         [Doctor] _exits._

1   *'Tis called the evil.*

    The practice of touching for the
    King's Evil, a disease characterized
    by the inflammation of the lymph
    nodes, was thought to have
    originated with Edward the
    Confessor and was continued by
    later English monarchs including
    Elizabeth I and James I. This ritual
    advertisement of the healing
    power of the royal touch was part
    of a more general cult of sacred
    monarchy. However, James was
    uncomfortable with the practice
    and was especially concerned to
    avoid the suggestion that cures
    were "miracles," precisely the
    interpretation that Malcolm
    encourages (4.3.147).

2   *strangely visited people*

    People afflicted with this unusual
    disease

3   *succeeding royalty*

    Monarchs that succeed him

Macduff T
What's the disease he means?
Malcolm (D's Son)
                                        'Tis called the evil. [1]
A most miraculous work in this good King,
stay   Which often since my here-remain° in England
induces the aid of   I have seen him do. How he solicits° Heaven
                          Himself best knows, but strangely visited people, [2]   150
                          All swoll'n and ulcerous, pitiful to the eye,
complete / medical treatment The mere° despair of surgery,° he cures,
coin   Hanging a golden stamp° about their necks,
                          Put on with holy prayers; and, 'tis spoken,
bequeaths   To the succeeding royalty [3] he leaves°   155
power   The healing benediction. With this strange virtue,°
                          He hath a heavenly gift of prophecy,
                          And sundry blessings hang about his throne
divine blessing   That speak him full of grace.°

                          Enter **Ross**. T

Macduff T
                                        See; who comes here?
Malcolm (D's Son)
recognize   My countryman, but yet I know° him not.   160
Macduff T
My ever-gentle cousin, welcome hither.
Malcolm (D's son)
quickly   I know him now.—Good God betimes° remove
                          The means that makes us strangers!
Ross T
                                        Sir, amen.

Macduff T
Stands Scotland where it did?

1   *modern ecstasy*
    Commonplace emotion

2   *The dead man's knell / Is there scarce*
    asked for who
    Hardly anyone asks for whom the
    death knell is sounded.

3   *or ere they sicken*
    Before they become ill

4   *That of an hour's age doth hiss the*
    speaker. / Each minute teems a new one.
    I.e., even news only an hour old is
    considered old news, and causes
    the person reporting it to be
    mocked. Every minute produces a
    new horror (*grief*).

Ross T

                                                   Alas, poor country,

Almost afraid to know itself! It cannot   165

no one   Be called our mother, but our grave, where nothing°

he who / ever   But who° knows nothing is once° seen to smile;

Where sighs and groans and shrieks that rend the air

noticed   Are made, not marked;° where violent sorrow seems

A modern ecstasy.[1] The dead man's knell   170

Is there scarce asked for who,[2] and good men's lives

Expire before the flowers in their caps,

Dying or ere they sicken.[3]

Macduff T

report   Oh, relation°

detailed   Too nice° and yet too true!

Malcolm (Ɔs sʊn)

(cause for) grief   What's the newest grief?°

Ross T

That of an hour's age doth hiss the speaker.   175

Each minute teems a new one.[4]

Macduff T

                                  How does my wife?

Ross T

Why, well.

Macduff T

              And all my children?

Ross T

                               Well too.

Macduff T

The tyrant has not battered at their peace?

Ross T

No, they were well at peace when I did leave 'em.

Macduff T

miser   Be not a niggard° of your speech. How goes 't?   180

1   *witnessed the rather / For that*
    Proven all the more because

2   *gives out*
    Proclaims

3   *fee-grief / Due to some single breast*
    **Personal grief belonging to a
    single individual. The term *fee-grief*
    seems to have been invented by
    Shakespeare, on the model of *fee-
    simple*, an estate belonging to one
    person and his heirs.**

Ross

news   When I came hither to transport the tidings,°
sadly   Which I have heavily° borne, there ran a rumor
on the battlefield Of many worthy fellows that were out,°
                Which was to my belief witnessed the rather
army   For that¹ I saw the tyrant's power° afoot.   185
for / appearance Now is the time of° help. [*to* **Malcolm**] Your eye° in
                     Scotland
                Would create soldiers, make our women fight,
cast off   To doff° their dire distresses.

Malcolm (D's Son)

                              Be 't their comfort
                We are coming thither. Gracious England hath
                Lent us good Siward and ten thousand men—   190
there is none An older and a better soldier none°
                That Christendom gives out.²

Ross

                              Would I could answer
                This comfort with the like. But I have words
should   That would° be howled out in the desert air,
catch   Where hearing should not latch° them.

Macduff

                                    What concern they? 195
                The general cause, or is it a fee-grief
                Due to some single breast?³

Ross

                              No mind that's honest
                But in it shares some woe, though the main part
                Pertains to you alone.

Macduff

                              If it be mine,
                Keep it not from me. Quickly let me have it.   200

1   *on the quarry of these murdered deer, /*
To add the death of you
To add your own death to the pile
of dead creatures

2   *pull your hat upon your brows*
I.e., hide your grief

3   *He*
It is unclear to whom *He* refers: if
Macbeth, his lack of children
means that Macduff cannot exact
parallel revenge; if Malcolm, it
explains why he does not fully
understand Macduff's grief.

4   *hell-kite*
Bird of Hell

Ross T

Let not your ears despise my tongue forever,

i.e., burden Which shall possess° them with the heaviest sound

That ever yet they heard.

Macduff T

Hum! I guess at it.

Ross T

attacked Your castle is surprised,° your wife and babes

Savagely slaughtered. To relate the manner   205

Were, on the quarry of these murdered deer,

To add the death of you. ¹

Malcolm (D's son)

Merciful Heaven!

What, man! Ne'er pull your hat upon your brows. ²

Give sorrow words. The grief that does not speak

Whispers to / overwhelmed Whispers° the o'erfraught° heart and bids it break.   210

Macduff T

My children too?

Ross T

Wife, children, servants—all that could be found.

Macduff T

had to And I must° be from thence!

My wife killed too?

Ross T

I have said.

Malcolm (D's son)

Be comforted.

Let's make us med'cines of our great revenge   215

To cure this deadly grief.

Macduff T

He ³ has no children. All my pretty ones?

Did you say "all"? O hell-kite! ⁴ All?

1   *But I must also feel it as a man*

According to Holinshed, Macduff was planning to leave for England when Macbeth assaulted his castle and killed his wife and child. Macduff was not there at the time, and in the aftermath he escaped to England. By rearranging the sequence of events, Shakespeare raises questions about Macduff's judgment, but also creates an occasion for Macduff's notable display of grief. Macduff's insistence that he must *feel it as a man* presents a masculinity that is tempered by sympathy and love for others.

2   *I cannot but remember such things were*

I cannot forget those things existed.

3   *take their part*

act on their behalf

4   *for*

Because of; instead of

5   *Oh, I could play the woman with mine eyes / And braggart with my tongue!*

I.e., oh, I could weep like a woman and bluster, boasting what I will do!

6   *Front to front*

Face to face

7   *Our lack is nothing but our leave*

We need only to say good-bye

8   *Put on their instruments*

(1) set us in motion (as their instruments); (2) arm themselves

mother   What, all my pretty chickens and their dam°
savage   At one fell° swoop?
Malcolm (D 's son)
Deal with   Dispute° it like a man.   220
Macduff
I shall do so,
But I must also feel it as a man.[1]
I cannot but remember such things were[2]
That were most precious to me. Did Heaven look on
And would not take their part?[3] Sinful Macduff,   225
Wicked person They were all struck for[4] thee! Naught° that I am,
Not for their own demerits, but for mine,
Fell slaughter on their souls. Heaven rest them now.
Malcolm (D'S son)
Be this the whetstone of your sword. Let grief
Transform itself Convert° to anger. Blunt not the heart; enrage it.   230
Macduff
Oh, I could play the woman with mine eyes
And braggart with my tongue![5] But, gentle heavens,
interval Cut short all intermission.° Front to front[6]
Bring thou this fiend of Scotland and myself.
escape Within my sword's length set him; if he 'scape,°   235
Heaven forgive him too.
Malcolm (D'S son)
                          This time goes manly.
army Come; go we to the King. Our power° is ready;
Our lack is nothing but our leave.[7] Macbeth
Is ripe for shaking, and the powers above
Put on their instruments.[8] Receive what cheer you may.   240
The night is long that never finds the day.   *They exit.*

1   *waiting* **Gentlewoman**
    An aristocratic woman who waits
    on the queen

2   *do the effects of watching*
    Carry on as though awake

3   *very guise*
    Usual behavior

Act 5, Scene 1

Enter a **Doctor** *of Physic and a waiting* **Gentlewoman**.[1]

(serving lady Macbeth)

Doctor

I have two nights watched with you but can perceive no
truth in your report. When was it she last walked?

Gentlewoman

battlefield   Since his Majesty went into the field,° I have seen her
dressing gown   rise from her bed, throw her nightgown° upon her,
cabinet   unlock her closet,° take forth paper, fold it, write upon   5
't, read it, afterwards seal it, and again return to bed;
yet all this while in a most fast sleep.

Doctor

disorder   A great perturbation° in nature, to receive at once the
benefit of sleep and do the effects of watching.[2] In this
movement   slumb'ry agitation,° besides her walking and other   10
active   actual° performances, what, at any time, have you
heard her say?

Gentlewoman

That, sir, which I will not report after her.

Doctor

appropriate   You may to me, and 'tis most meet° you should.

Gentlewoman

Neither to you nor any one, having no witness to   15
confirm my speech.

Enter **Lady [Macbeth]**, *with a taper.*

Lo you, here she comes. This is her very guise,[3] and,
out of sight   upon my life, fast asleep. Observe her; stand close.°

Doctor

How came she by that light?

1   *One, two.*

Presumably, she is counting the
strikes of the clock, as she may
have done on the night of the
murder; see 2.1.62.

Gentlewoman

Why, it stood by her. She has light by her continually;   20
'Tis her command.

Doctor

You see her eyes are open.

Gentlewoman

Ay, but their sense are shut.

Doctor

What is it she does now? Look how she rubs her hands.

Gentlewoman

customary It is an accustomed° action with her to seem thus   25
washing her hands. I have known her continue in this a
quarter of an hour.

Lady Macbeth

Yet here's a spot.

Doctor

write Hark! She speaks. I will set° down what comes from her
reinforce to satisfy° my remembrance the more strongly.   30

Lady Macbeth

Out, damned spot! Out, I say! One, two. ¹ Why, then,
'tis time to do 't. Hell is murky!—Fie, my lord, fie! A
soldier, and afeard? What need we fear who knows it,
when none can call our power to account?—Yet who
would have thought the old man to have had so much   35
blood in him.

Doctor

Do you mark that?

Lady Macbeth

The Thane of Fife had a wife. Where is she now?—
What, will these hands ne'er be clean?—No more o'
everything that, my lord, no more o' that. You mar all° with this   40
fitfulness starting.°

1   *Go to*
     **I.e., for shame (mild expression of
     reproach)**

2   *sorely charged*
     Heavily burdened

Doctor

Go to, [1] go to. You have known what you should not.

Gentlewoman

She has spoke what she should not; I am sure of that.
Heaven knows what she has known.

Lady Macbeth

Here's the smell of the blood still. All the perfumes of   45
Arabia will not sweeten this little hand. Oh, oh, oh.

Doctor

What a sigh is there! The heart is sorely charged. [2]

Gentlewoman

I would not have such a heart in my bosom for the
status (as queen)   dignity° of the whole body.

Doctor

Well, well, well.   50

Gentlewoman

Pray God it be, sir.

Doctor

skill   This disease is beyond my practice.° Yet I have known
those which have walked in their sleep who have died
holily in their beds.

Lady Macbeth

Wash your hands. Put on your nightgown. Look not so   55
pale.—I tell you yet again, Banquo's buried; he cannot
of   come out on° 's grave.

Doctor

Even so?

Lady Macbeth

To bed, to bed. There's knocking at the gate. Come,
come, come, come. Give me your hand. What's done   60
cannot be undone. To bed, to bed, to bed!

Lady [*Macbeth*] *exits.*

1   *I think but dare not speak.*

The doctor now knows of the
regicide but is afraid to speak of it.

Doctor
Will she go now to bed?

Gentlewoman
Directly.

Doctor
Foul whisp'rings are abroad. Unnatural deeds
Do breed unnatural troubles. Infected minds   65
To their deaf pillows will discharge their secrets.
priest More needs she the divine° than the physician.
God, God forgive us all! Look after her.
injury (to herself) Remove from her the means of all annoyance,°
always And still° keep eyes upon her. So, good night.   70
bewildered My mind she has mated,° and amazed my sight.
I think but dare not speak. [1]

Gentlewoman
                                      Good night, good doctor.

                                                    They exit.

1 Drum and colors.

    I.e., drummers and flagbearers.

2 *their dear causes / Would to the bleeding*
    and the grim alarm / Excite the mortified
    man

    Their grievous wrongs would
    awaken the dead to answer the call
    to deadly battle.

3 *Protest their first of manhood*

    Declare themselves of age for this
    first act of manhood

4 *He cannot buckle his distempered cause /*
    Within the belt of rule

    I.e., Macbeth's ambition has
    gotten so out of hand that he can
    no longer restrain himself.
    Caithness describes Macbeth's
    cause **as a** *distempered* **(diseased and**
    distended) belly, which can no
    longer be contained by a *belt.*

5 *upbraid his faith-breach*

    Reproach his treason

6 *in command*

    Because they are under order

Act 5, Scene 2

Drum and colors. [1]

Enter **Menteith**, **Caithness**, **Angus**, **Lennox**, [*and*] *soldiers.*

Menteith (Thanes)

army The English power° is near, led on by Malcolm,
His uncle Siward, and the good Macduff.
Revenges burn in them, for their dear causes
Would to the bleeding and the grim alarm
Excite the mortified man. [2]

Angus

Near Birnam Wood 5

undoubtedly Shall we well° meet them. That way are they coming.

Caithness

Who knows if Donalbain be with his brother?

Lennox

list For certain, sir, he is not: I have a file°
Of all the gentry. There is Siward's son
smooth-faced; young And many unrough° youths that even now 10
Protest their first of manhood. [3]

Menteith

What does the tyrant?

Caithness

Great Dunsinane he strongly fortifies.
Some say he's mad; others, that lesser hate him,
Do call it valiant fury. But, for certain,
diseased; distended He cannot buckle his distempered° cause 15
Within the belt of rule. [4]

Angus

Now does he feel
His secret murders sticking on his hands.
by the minute Now minutely° revolts upbraid his faith-breach. [5]
Those he commands move only in command, [6]

1   *med'cine*

    I.e., Malcolm; note the *med'cines* of
    revenge that Malcolm encouraged
    Macduff to make (see 4.3.215)

2   *dew the sovereign flower*

    Water the legitimate flower.
    Lennox no doubt means that this
    will be done in blood. *Sovereign* = (1)
    royal; (2) potentially medicinal

Nothing in love. Now does he feel his title 20
Hang loose about him, like a giant's robe
Upon a dwarfish thief.

Menteith   ⊤
                                Who, then, shall blame

vexed; troubled His pestered° senses to recoil and start,
When all that is within him does condemn
Itself for being there?

Caithness   ⊤
                                Well, march we on 25
To give obedience where 'tis truly owed.

state Meet we the med'cine[1] of the sickly weal,°
And with him pour we in our country's purge,
Each drop of us.

Lennox   ⊤
                        Or so much as it needs
To dew the sovereign flower[2] and drown the weeds. 30
Make we our march towards Birnam.

                                They exit, marching.

1   *Let them fly all.*

Let all the thanes flee. (Presumably
all the *reports* are of desertions.)

2   *mortal consequences*

(1) human eventualities; (2) fatal
outcomes

3   *epicures*

Those who live for sensual
pleasure; Holinshed reports the
Scottish scorn of English luxury.

4   *over-red thy fear*

Make your cheeks red (to rid
yourself of that cowardly pallor).

5   *lily-livered*

I.e., pale-livered, cowardly (the *liver*
was thought to be the source of
courage).

6   *Are counselors to fear*

Teach others to be afraid

7   *linen cheeks . . . whey-face*

Macbeth uses various images of pale
coloring (*cream, linen, whey*) to
express his contempt of cowardice
that robs the face of its natural color
(*whey* = the watery part of milk).

Act 5, Scene 3

*Enter **Macbeth**, **Doctor**, and attendants.*

Macbeth

Bring me no more reports. Let them fly all. [1]
Till Birnam Wood remove to Dunsinane
become infected I cannot taint° with fear. What's the boy Malcolm?
Was he not born of woman? The spirits that know
All mortal consequences [2] have pronounced me thus: 5
"Fear not, Macbeth. No man that's born of woman
Shall e'er have power upon thee." Then fly, false
   thanes,
And mingle with the English epicures. [3]
govern myself The mind I sway° by and the heart I bear
Shall never sag with doubt nor shake with fear.   10

*Enter **Servant**.*

rogue The devil damn thee black, thou cream-faced loon!°
Where got'st thou that goose look?
Servant
There is ten thousand—
Macbeth

          Geese, villain?
Servant

            Soldiers, sir.
Macbeth

Go prick thy face and over-red thy fear, [4]
fool Thou lily-livered [5] boy. What soldiers, patch?°   15
on Death of° thy soul! Those linen cheeks of thine
Are counselors to fear. [6] What soldiers, whey-face? [7]
Servant
The English force, so please you.

1   *cheer me ever*

    Both "comfort me forever" and, punning on the words *cheer* and *chair*, "keep me enthroned forever."

2   *the yellow leaf*

    I.e., the dying leaf of autumn

3   *mouth-honor*

    I.e., respect from people's lips (but not their hearts)

Macbeth

Take thy face hence. [**Servant** exits.] Seyton!—I am
  sick at heart,

effort When I behold—Seyton, I say!—This push°   20

dethrone Will cheer me ever¹ or disseat° me now.

I have lived long enough. My way of life

withered condition Is fall'n into the sere,° the yellow leaf,²

And that which should accompany old age,

Such as As° honor, love, obedience, troops of friends,   25

I must not look to have, but in their stead

Curses, not loud but deep, mouth-honor,³ breath

gladly Which the poor heart would fain° deny and dare not.

Seyton!

Enter **Seyton**. (officer serving macbeth)

Seyton

What's your gracious pleasure?

Macbeth

                              What news more?   30

Seyton

All is confirmed, my lord, which was reported.

Macbeth

I'll fight till from my bones my flesh be hacked.

Give me my armor.

Seyton

                  'Tis not needed yet.

Macbeth

I'll put it on.

Scour Send out more horses. Skirr° the country round.   35

1 *thick-coming fancies*

Frequent hallucinations

2 *Raze out the written troubles of*

Rub out the troubles inscribed in

3 *stuff*

Substance. The near repetition of *stuffed* earlier in the line has led some editors to suggest this is an error, but perhaps the point is that the beleaguered Macbeth cannot be bothered to find a more exact term.

4 *send out*

I.e., the horses, as he was commanded in line 5.3.35

5 *cast / The water of my land*

I.e., make a diagnosis of Scotland's illness by examining its urine

6 *Pull 't off, I say.*

I.e., the armor. Perhaps Macbeth has changed his mind again, or perhaps one piece was put on incorrectly.

7 *rhubarb, senna*

Both medicinal plants; herbalists sometimes recommend mixing these to produce a purgative.

Hang those that talk of fear. Give me mine armor.

How does your patient, doctor?

Doctor

                          Not so sick, my lord,

As she is troubled with thick-coming fancies [1]

That keep her from her rest.

Macbeth

                             Cure her of that.

Canst thou not minister to a mind diseased,   40

Pluck from the memory a rooted sorrow,

Raze out the written troubles of [2] the brain,

inducing forgetfulness And with some sweet oblivious° antidote

i.e., clogged Cleanse the stuffed° bosom of that perilous stuff [3]

Which weighs upon the heart?

Doctor

                         Therein the patient   45

Must minister to himself.

Macbeth

(practice of) medicine Throw physic° to the dogs; I'll none of it.

spear —Come, put mine armor on. Give me my staff.°

Seyton, send out. [4]—Doctor, the thanes fly from me.

hurry up —Come, sir, dispatch.°—If thou couldst, doctor, cast   50

The water of my land, [5] find her disease,

And purge it to a sound and pristine health,

I would applaud thee to the very echo,

That should applaud again.—Pull 't off, I say. [6]

—What rhubarb, senna, [7] or what purgative drug,   55

remove; clear out Would scour° these English hence? Hear'st thou of

i.e., the English   them?°

Doctor

Ay, my good lord. Your royal preparation

Makes us hear something.

1   *Profit again should hardly draw me here*

Not even a large profit could
convince me to return here (a joke
about the proverbial greed of
doctors).

Macbeth

i.e., the armor   Bring it° after me.

ruin   I will not be afraid of death and bane°

Till Birnam Forest come to Dunsinane.   60

Doctor

[*aside*] Were I from Dunsinane away and clear,

Profit again should hardly draw me here. ¹   *They exit.*

1   *chambers*
    Household rooms, such as dining
    rooms or bedchambers; perhaps a
    reference to Duncan's assassination

2   *no other but*
    Nothing but that

3   *setting down before 't*
    Laying siege in front of it

4   *where there is advantage to be given, /*
    Both more and less have given him the
    revolt
    The sense is, "Even where he has
    the opportunity for some military
    advantage, both nobles and
    commoners have deserted him."

Act 5, Scene 4

Drum and colors. Enter **Malcolm, Siward, Macduff,**
Siward's son, Menteith, Caithness, Angus, [**Lennox,**
Ross,] *and* **Soldiers,** *marching.*

Malcolm

Kinsmen   Cousins,° I hope the days are near at hand

That chambers¹ will be safe.

Menteith

not at all   We doubt it nothing.°

Siward

What wood is this before us?

Menteith

                                        The wood of Birnam.

Malcolm

cut   Let every soldier hew° him down a bough

hide   And bear 't before him. Thereby shall we shadow°   5

army / reconnaissance   The numbers of our host° and make discovery°

Err in report of us.

Soldiers

                    It shall be done.

Siward

We learn no other but² the confident tyrant

Keeps still in Dunsinane and will endure

Our setting down before 't.³

Malcolm

                                        'Tis his main hope,   10

For where there is advantage to be given,

Both more and less have given him the revolt,⁴

And none serve with him but constrainèd things

Whose hearts are absent too.

1   *Thoughts speculative their unsure hopes*
    relate, / But certain issue strokes must
    arbitrate

    **In anticipation we voice our
    unreliable optimism, but the true
    outcome will be decided by blows.**

Macduff ~Thane~

evaluations   Let our just censures°

outcome   Attend the true event,° and put we on   15

Industrious soldiership.

Siward ~earl~

The time approaches

That will with due decision make us know

(in fact) own   What we shall say we have and what we owe.°

Thoughts speculative their unsure hopes relate,

But certain issue strokes must arbitrate [1]—   20

i.e., troops   Towards which, advance the war.°   *They exit, marching.*

1 *laugh a siege to scorn*

   A reference to the witches' earlier injunction to *Laugh to scorn / The power of man*, in 4.1.79–80.

2 *those that should be ours*

   I.e., deserters, traitors

3 *my senses would have cooled*

   I would have been chilled with fear.

4 *supped full with*

   Eaten my fill of

Act 5, Scene 5

Enter **Macbeth**, **Seyton**, *and* **Soldiers**, *with drum and colors.*

Macbeth   *officr serving macbeth*

Hang out our banners on the outward walls.
The cry is still "They come!" Our castle's strength
Will laugh a siege to scorn. [1] Here let them lie

fever   Till famine and the ague° eat them up.
reinforced   Were they not forced° with those that should be ours, [2]   5
boldly   We might have met them dareful,° beard to beard,
And beat them backward home.   *A cry within of women.*

                    What is that noise?

Seyton

It is the cry of women, my good lord.   [*He exits.*]

Macbeth

I have almost forgot the taste of fears.
The time has been my senses would have cooled [3]   10

shock   To hear a night-shriek, and my fell° of hair
story   Would at a dismal treatise° rouse and stir
As if   As° life were in 't. I have supped full with [4] horrors.
Horror   Direness,° familiar to my slaughterous thoughts
startle   Cannot once start° me.

         [*Enter* **Seyton**.]

For what reason   Wherefore° was that cry?   15

Seyton

The Queen, my lord, is dead.

1   *She should have died hereafter.*

She should have died at some later
time, either so that she would live
a full life, or so that she should die
when there was more time to
mourn her. There is a possible
alternate sense: "She would
certainly have died eventually."
Taken with *There would have been a
time*, the former is probably more
appropriate, but given the sense of
the subsequent soliloquy, the
latter is not impossible.

2   *a walking shadow, a poor player*

Shadow and *player* are being used
both in general senses, pointing to
the insubstantiality of human life,
and in their specific application to
stage actors. *Fools*, in line 5.5.21,
also has this double sense.

Macbeth

                              She should have died hereafter. [1]

(i.e., "dead")   There would have been a time for such a word.°

                    Tomorrow, and tomorrow, and tomorrow

insignificant (i.e., slow)   Creeps in this petty° pace from day to day

                    To the last syllable of recorded time,   20

                    And all our yesterdays have lighted fools

                    The way to dusty death. Out, out, brief candle!

                    Life's but a walking shadow, a poor player [2]

                    That struts and frets his hour upon the stage

                    And then is heard no more. It is a tale   25

                    Told by an idiot, full of sound and fury,

                    Signifying nothing.

                    Enter a **Messenger**.

                              Thou com'st to use

                    Thy tongue; thy story quickly.

                    Messenger

                              Gracious my lord,

                    I should report that which I say I saw,

                    But know not how to do 't.

Macbeth

                              Well, say, sir.   30

                    Messenger

                    As I did stand my watch upon the hill,

suddenly   I looked toward Birnam and anon° methought

                    The wood began to move.

Macbeth

                              Liar and slave!

1   *pull in resolution*

Rein in my confidence

2   *estate*

Make up; state; order

Messenger

Let me endure your wrath if 't be not so.

Within this three mile may you see it coming,   35

I say, a moving grove.

Macbeth

                        If thou speak'st false,

Upon the next tree shall thou hang alive

shrivel / truth   Till famine cling° thee. If thy speech be sooth,°

I care not if thou dost for me as much.

I pull in resolution [1] and begin   40

fear; suspect   To doubt° th' equivocation of the fiend

That lies like truth. "Fear not till Birnam Wood

Do come to Dunsinane," and now a wood

To arms   Comes toward Dunsinane.—Arm,° arm, and out!

claims   —If this which he avouches° does appear,   45

There is nor flying hence nor tarrying here.

I 'gin to be aweary of the sun,

And wish th' estate [2] o' th' world were now undone.

ruin   —Ring the alarum-bell! —Blow, wind! Come, wrack!°

armor   At least we'll die with harness° on our back.   *They exit.*   50

1 *we*

Malcolm has assumed the
prerogative of the royal *we*.

2 *Do we but*

If we should

Act 5, Scene 6

Drum and colors.

Enter **Malcolm**, **Siward**, **Macduff**, *and their army, with boughs.* (D's son) (earl) (Thane)

Malcolm D's son

Now near enough. Your leafy screens throw down

appear / i.e., Siward   And show° like those you are.—You, worthy uncle,°

Shall, with my cousin, your right-noble son,

division   Lead our first battle.° Worthy Macduff and we [1]

Shall take upon 's what else remains to do,   5

battle plan   According to our order.°

Siward earl

              Fare you well.

army   Do we but [2] find the tyrant's power° tonight,

Let us be beaten if we cannot fight.

Macduff T

Make all our trumpets speak; give them all breath,

Those clamorous harbingers of blood and death.   10

                        They exit.

                   Alarums continued.

1   *They have tied me to a stake. I cannot fly, /*
    But, bearlike, I must fight the course.

    The image is from bear-baiting, a
    sport in which a bear was tied to a
    stake and dogs were set to attack it.
    A *course* was the attack by the dogs.

Act 5, Scene 7

Enter **Macbeth**.

Macbeth

They have tied me to a stake. I cannot fly,
But, bearlike, I must fight the course. ¹ What's he
That was not born of woman? Such a one
Am I to fear, or none.

Enter **Young Siward**.

Young Siward *earl's son*

What is thy name?   5

Macbeth

Thou 'lt be afraid to hear it.

Young Siward

No, though thou call'st thyself a hotter name
that is Than any is° in Hell.

Macbeth

My name's Macbeth.

Young Siward

The devil himself could not pronounce a title
More hateful to mine ear.

Macbeth

No, nor more fearful.   10

Young Siward

Thou liest, abhorrèd tyrant. With my sword
prove false I'll prove° the lie thou speak'st.

[*They*] *fight, and* **Young Siward** [*is*] *slain.*

1   *laugh to scorn*

    Another reference to the witches'
    prophecy at 4.1.79–80, where the
    sisters tell Macbeth to *Laugh to scorn /
    The power of man.*

2   He exits

    Macbeth must take Young Siward's
    body with him. If left on stage, it
    would have to remain there for the
    rest of the play. The staging would
    then have to make plausible
    Macduff and Siward's failure to
    notice the body, which might also
    prove a physical obstacle in the
    subsequent fight scene.

3   *undeeded*

    Having done nothing

4   *one of greatest note / Seems bruited*

    One worthy of great notice seems
    to be announced

Macbeth

> Thou wast born of woman.
> But swords I smile at, weapons laugh to scorn, [1]
> Brandished by man that's of a woman born. *He exits.* [2]
> *Alarums.*

Enter **Macduff**. Thane

Macduff T

	That way the noise is. Tyrant, show thy face! 15
by	If thou bee'st slain, and with° no stroke of mine,
always	My wife and children's ghosts will haunt me still.°
hired soldiers	I cannot strike at wretched kerns,° whose arms
spears	Are hired to bear their staves.° Either thou, Macbeth,
	Or else my sword with an unbattered edge 20
	I sheathe again undeeded. [3] There thou shouldst be;
	By this great clatter, one of greatest note
	Seems bruited. [4] Let me find him, Fortune,
	And more I beg not. *He exits. Alarums.*

Enter **Malcolm** *and* **Siward**.

Siward earl

surrendered	This way, my lord. The castle's gently 'rendered.° 25
	The tyrant's people on both sides do fight,
	The noble thanes do bravely in the war,
proclaims itself	The day almost itself professes° yours,
	And little is to do.

1   *foes / That strike beside us*

    (1) foes who turn and take our side;

    (2) foes who miss on purpose

Malcolm

We have met with foes

That strike beside us. [1]

Siward *earl*

Enter, sir, the castle. 30

They exit. Alarums.

1   *play the Roman fool and die / On mine*
    own sword
    Commit suicide by falling on my
    own sword (following the Roman
    code of honor), rather than admit
    defeat

2   *terms can give thee out*
    Can be put in words

3   *losest labor*
    Expend unnecessary effort

Act 5, Scene 8

Enter **Macbeth**.

Macbeth

Why should I play the Roman fool and die

living beings On mine own sword?¹ Whiles I see lives,° the gashes

Do better upon them.

Enter **Macduff**.

Macduff ⌐

                             Turn, hellhound, turn!

Macbeth

Of all men else I have avoided thee.

But get thee back. My soul is too much charged   5

With blood of thine already.

Macduff ⌐

                          I have no words.

My voice is in my sword. Thou bloodier villain

Than terms can give thee out!²

                          [They] fight. Alarums.

Macbeth

                     Thou losest labor.³

invulnerable As easy mayst thou the intrenchant° air

sharp / mark With thy keen° sword impress° as make me bleed.   10

i.e., heads Let fall thy blade on vulnerable crests.°

I bear a charmèd life, which must not yield

To one of woman born.

Macduff ⌐

Despair of   Despair° thy charm,

1   *Macduff was from his mother's womb/*
    Untimely ripped

    A caesarean birth would have been
    performed by male surgeons, as
    opposed to female midwives, and
    it would also likely have resulted in
    the death of the mother. Medical
    experts disagreed over whether or
    not the procedure should be
    performed upon a living mother.
    Helikiah Crooke, a physician and
    anatomist, writes, "If the mother
    be dead and the child yet living,
    then presently without any delay
    the womb of the mother must be
    ripped open . . . But if the mother
    yet be alive and the infant by no
    other means can safely be brought
    forth, the same section or opening
    of the womb may be administered;
    for common experience and the
    authority of ancient Physicians do
    assure us that the wounds of the
    muscles of the lower belly and of
    the *Peritoneum* or rim are not
    mortal." The French physician
    James Guillimeau, on the other
    hand, argues that the procedure
    should only be used once the
    mother has died.

2   *my better part of man*

    The larger proportion of my
    manhood (i.e., more than half of
    my courage)

3   *We'll have thee, as our rarer monsters*
    are, / Painted upon a pole

    I.e., we'll have your image (like
    some unusual monster) painted
    on a sign as an advertisement (in
    front of a carnival booth)

4   *try the last*

    Wait for the outcome; test the end

i.e., evil spirit / always   And let the angel° whom thou still° hast served

Tell thee Macduff was from his mother's womb   15

Untimely ripped. [1]

Macbeth

Accursèd be that tongue that tells me so,

intimidated   For it hath cowed° my better part of man! [2]

And be these juggling fiends no more believed

equivocate   That palter° with us in a double sense,   20

That keep the word of promise to our ear

And break it to our hope. I'll not fight with thee.

Macduff

Then yield thee, coward,

spectacle   And live to be the show and gaze° o' th' time.

curiosities   We'll have thee, as our rarer monsters° are,   25

written underneath   Painted upon a pole, [3] and underwrit,°

"Here may you see the tyrant."

Macbeth

I will not yield

To kiss the ground before young Malcolm's feet,

taunted   And to be baited° with the rabble's curse.

Though Birnam Wood be come to Dunsinane,   30

And thou opposed, being of no woman born,

Yet I will try the last. [4] Before my body

I throw my warlike shield. Lay on, Macduff,

And damned be him that first cries, "Hold,

enough!"   *They exit, fighting. Alarums.*

[They] enter fighting, and **Macbeth** *[is] slain.*

*[***Macduff*** *exits, with* **Macbeth**'s *body.*

1   *go off*
    Die

2   *unshrinking station*
    **I.e., position that he did not
    surrender**

3   *knell is knolled*
    **Death knell is rung on the church
    bell**

Retreat and flourish. Enter, with drum and colors,
Malcolm, Siward, Ross, Thanes, *and*
Soldiers.

Malcolm

wish   I would° the friends we miss were safe arrived.   35

Siward *earl*

those here   Some must go off,[1] and yet, by these° I see

So great a day as this is cheaply bought.

Malcolm

Macduff is missing, and your noble son.

Ross T

Your son, my lord, has paid a soldier's debt.

He only lived but till he was a man,   40

The which no sooner had his prowess confirmed

In the unshrinking station[2] where he fought,

But like a man he died.

Siward *earl*

         Then he is dead?

Ross T

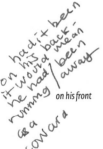

Ay, and brought off the field. Your cause of sorrow

Must not be measured by his worth, for then   45

It hath no end.

Siward *earl*

on his front   Had he his hurts before?°

Ross T

Ay, on the front.

Siward *earl*

         Why then, God's soldier be he!

Had I as many sons as I have hairs,

I would not wish them to a fairer death.

And so his knell is knolled.[3]

1   *stands*

Macbeth's head *stands* on a pike or
lance.

2   *The time is free.*

The age, or the land, is *free* from
Macbeth's tyrrany.

3   *kingdom's pearl*

I.e., the nobles of the kingdom

4   *make us even with you*

Repay our debts to you

5   *Henceforth be earls, the first that ever
Scotland / In such an honor named*

This detail is supplied by
Holinshed: Malcolm rewards many
of his followers by creating them
earls: "These were the first earls
that have been heard of amongst
the Scotishmen (as their histories
do make mention)." The rank of
earl was, in post-Conquest
England, considered the
equivalent of count, a European
title. The transformation of
Malcolm's *thanes and kinsmen* into
earls alludes to the long historical
process of Anglicization by which
England attempted to impose its
culture on Scotland. Compare
Macbeth's proper Scottish
contempt for the *English epicures*
(5.3.8).

6   *Which would be planted newly with the
time*

Which should be carried out to
commence this new age (and the
image of planting marks the
restitution of order after Macbeth's
unnatural rule)

7   *Producing forth*

Bring out of hiding (i.e., to put on
trial)

Malcolm

                             He's worth more sorrow,   50

And that I'll spend for him.

Siward *earl*

                           He's worth no more.

departed / debt   They say he parted° well and paid his score,°

And so God be with him! Here comes newer comfort.

Enter **Macduff**, *with* **Macbeth**'s *head.*

Macduff T

Hail, King, for so thou art. Behold where stands [1]

Th' usurper's cursèd head. The time is free. [2]   55

surrounded   I see thee compassed° with thy kingdom's pearl, [3]

That speak my salutation in their minds,

Whose voices I desire aloud with mine.

Hail, King of Scotland!

All

                      Hail, King of Scotland!

                             Flourish.

Malcolm

We shall not spend a large expense of time   60

settle accounts / various   Before we reckon° with your several° loves

And make us even with you. [4] My thanes and kinsmen,

Henceforth be earls, the first that ever Scotland

In such an honor named. [5] What's more to do,

Which would be planted newly with the time, [6]   65

Such as   As° calling home our exiled friends abroad

That fled the snares of watchful tyranny,

agents   Producing forth [7] the cruel ministers°

1   *self and violent hands*

   Her own violent hands

2   *grace of grace*

   **The expected phrase, "by the grace
   of God," was a common feature in
   the styles of both English and
   Scottish monarchs.** *Grace* **itself is an
   important term in the play; see
   also,** *Renown and grace is dead*
   (2.3.92) and *Though all things foul
   would wear the brows of grace, / Yet
   grace must still look so* **(4.3.23–24).**

3   *in measure, time, and place*

   **In due proportion, at the
   appropriate time and place**

Of this dead butcher and his fiendlike queen—
Who, as 'tis thought, by self and violent hands[1]   70
Took off her life—this, and what needful else
That calls upon us, by the grace of grace,[2]
We will perform in measure, time, and place.[3]
So, thanks to all at once and to each one,
Whom we invite to see us crowned at Scone.   75

Flourish. They exit.

Appendix

(1) Near the end of Act Three, scene five, the 1673 Quarto of *Macbeth* prints the complete song merely indicated by the incipit in the Folio, which is printed on p. 183. What appears below is a modernized version of the 1673 text, though the song derives from Thomas Middleton's *The Witch* (written about 1610) and at some point soon after it was written seems to have been introduced into Shakespeare's play as it was performed by the King's Men.

[First Spirit]
Come away, Hecate, Hecate; Oh, come away.

[Hecate]
I come, I come, with all the speed I may;
I come, I come, with all the speed I may.

[First Spirit]
Where's Stadling?

[Second Spirit]
Here.

[Hecate]

Where's Puckle?

[Third Spirit]

Here; and Hopper too and Hellway too.

[First Spirit]

We want but you, we want but you.

Come away; make up the count.

[Hecate]

I will but 'noint and then I mount;

I will but 'noint and then I mount,

> [*A spirit like a cat descends.*]

[First Spirit]

Here comes one; it is

To fetch his due: a kiss,

Ay, a coll, a sip of blood;

And why thou stay'st so long, I muse,

Since the air's so sweet and good.

Oh art thou come? What news?

[Second Spirit]

All goes fair for our delight;

Either come, or else refuse.

[Hecate]

Now I am furnished for the flight.

Now I go; now I fly,

Malkin my sweet spirit and I.

> [*Hecate and the cat ascend.*]

[Third Spirit]

Oh, what a dainty pleasure's this,
To sail i' th' air
While the moon shines fair,
To sing, to toy and kiss;
Over woods, high rocks, and mountains,
Over misty hills and fountains,
Over steeples, towers, and turrets,
We fly by night 'mongst troops of spirits.

[Chorus of Spirits]

No ring of bells to our ears sounds,
No noise of wolves, nor yelps of hounds,
No, nor the noise of waters' breach,
Or cannon's throat our height can reach.   *They Exit.*

(2) In Act Four, scene one, the 1673 Quarto of *Macbeth* repeats the Folio incipit printed on p. 191. What is printed here is a modernized version of the song as it appears in Act Five, scene two of Middleton's *The Witch*.

[Hecate]

Black spirits and white, red spirits and gray,
Mingle, mingle, mingle, you that mingle may.
Titty, Tiffin, keep it stiff in.
Firedrake, Puckey, make it lucky;
Liard, Robin, you must bob in.

[Chorus of Witches]

Round, around, around, about, about;
All ill come running in, all good keep out.

[First Witch]

Here's the blood of a bat.

[Hecate]
Put in that; oh, put in that!

[Second Witch]
Here's leopard's bane.

[Hecate]
Put in again!

[First Witch]
The juice of toad, the oil of adder—

[Second Witch]
Those will make the younker madder!

[Hecate]
Put in. There's all, and rid the stench.

[Firestone]
Nay, here's three ounces of the red-haired wench.

[Chorus of Witches]
Round, around, around, about, about;
All ill come running in, all good keep out.

Longer Notes

1.4.39   *Prince of Cumberland*
According to Holinshed, Duncan
made Malcolm "prince of Cumberland, as it were thereby to appoint
him his successor in the kingdom,
immediately after his decease.
Macbeth sore troubled herewith, for
he saw by this means his hope sore
hindered (where, by the old laws of
the realm, the ordinance was, that
if he that should succeed were not
of able age to take the charge upon
himself, he that was next of blood
unto him should be admitted) he
began to take counsel how he might
usurp the kingdom by force, having
a just quarrel so to do (as he took
the matter) for that Duncan did
what in him lay to defraud him of all
manner of title and claim, which he
might in time to come, pretend unto

the crown." Shakespeare removes
Holinshed's hint that Macbeth had a
genuine grievance (the abrogation
of "old laws") and compresses
events so that Holinshed's short
interval in which Macbeth patiently
waits to become king disappears.

1.7.7   *jump the life to come*
The word *jump* in this phrase is most
commonly glossed as meaning
"risk," though contemporary
instances of the verb form of *jump*
being used in this way are quite rare
(the *Oxford English Dictionary* cites only
this passage and *Cymbeline* 5.4.188).
However, a noun form of the word
meaning, "the decisive moment of
plunging into action of doubtful
issue," or "venture, hazard, risk" is
common in late Elizabethan English.
Since Shakespeare frequently turns

nouns into verbs, the usual gloss may be correct. Nonetheless, the usual sense of the original verb—*to leap*—remains powerfully present. Interpretation is further complicated by the phrase *the life to come*. If this is taken to mean a heavenly afterlife, the phrase must mean "risk judgment in the next world after his life *here* on Earth." If *the life to come* refers to a future earthly existence, then either sense of *jump* works— Macbeth will leap over and out of life by setting in motion a sequence of events that will quickly lead to his death, or he will risk setting in motion such a sequence.

PAGE 91

1.7.25–28   *I have no spur / To prick the sides of my intent, but only / Vaulting ambition, which o'erleaps itself / And falls on th' other*
A vivid image that still causes confusion. Initially "Vaulting ambition" serves as a "spur to prick" the sides of his intent, which, to pursue the metaphor, assumes the place of a horse. But "Vaulting ambition" fails to land in the saddle instead falling on the far side of its mount. A more dignified alternative reads "Vaulting ambition" as a

horsed rider who attempts a jump too high or far and falls as a consequence. The difficulties occasioned by the "spur" and "vaulting" metaphors are typical of *Macbeth*. In the words of John Upton, an 18th-century critic, "Shakespeare laboring with a multiplicity of sublime ideas often gives himself not time to be delivered of them by the rules of *slow-endeavouring art*: hence he crowds various figures together, and metaphor upon metaphor; and runs the hazard of far-fetched expressions, whilst intent on nobler ideas he condescends not to grammatical niceties."

PAGE 103

2.1.33–34   *Is this a dagger which I see before me, / The handle toward my hand?*
In Shakespeare's time the most sustained attention to the problem of visual hallucinations and optical illusions was to be found in the literature concerning ghosts and witchcraft. Lewis Lavater's book, *Of Ghosts and Spirits Walking by Night* (1572), affirms that "spirits and sights do appear" but insists that they are not the souls of the dead but "either good or bad angels or

else some secret and hid operations." Le Loyer's *Treatise of Specters* (1605) devotes its opening section to definitions and makes a sharp distinction between phantasm and specter. The first is "an imagination of things which are not indeed, and doth proceed of the senses being corrupted"; the second is a substance without a body. In addition to the corruption of the senses, phantasms could be brought on by madness. As Gertrude says to Hamlet when he responds to a ghost that she can neither see nor hear: "This is the very coinage of your brain. / This bodiless creation ecstasy / Is very cunning in" (3.4.137–139). Yet another possibility is demonic interference; as Lavater observes, the devil "may easily deceive the eyesight and other senses of man."

PAGES 117 AND 119

2.3.8–11; 28–34 *an equivocator* The Porter's description of "an equivocator" alludes to the Gunpowder Plot of November 5, 1605, a failed attempt by a small group of English Catholics to blow up the king and Parliament. Father Henry Garnet, a Jesuit, had associated with several of the plotters and was quickly captured and imprisoned by a government eager to present the conspiracy as a Jesuit plot. Francis Tresham, one of the plotters, was discovered to have a manuscript written by Garnet, entitled A *Treatise of Equivocation*. It advocated not only giving ambiguous and evasive answers to interrogators but also defended the technique of mental reservation, in which one spoke words that had a misleading or false signification while adding a silent mental supplement that rendered the entire proposition truthful. Mental reservation had a long scholastic history, but in late 16th-century England it was identified almost exclusively with the Jesuits. Sir Edward Coke, the attorney general, made Garnet's *Treatise* a major part of the prosecution's case, and in the wake of the executions that followed the term *equivocation* became infamous. This topical allusion gives *equivocation* a peculiar charge, but the problem of ambiguous and deceitful language begins with "Fair is foul, and foul is fair" and runs through the entire play. Cf. "th' equivocation of the fiend" (5.5.41).

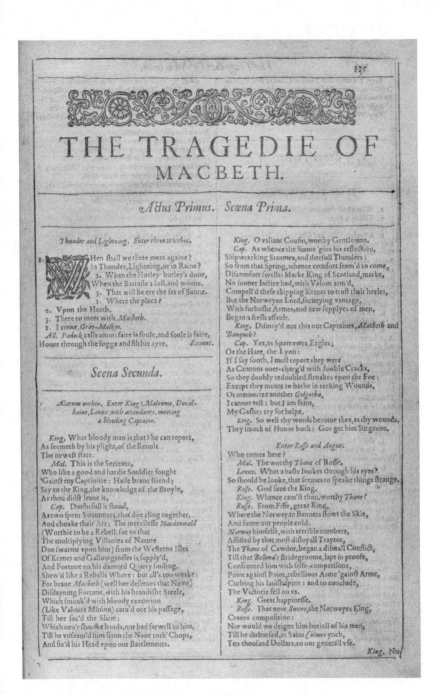

THE TRAGEDIE OF
MACBETH.

Actus Primus. Scœna Prima.

Thunder and Lightning. Enter three Witches.

1. Hen shall we three meet againe?
In Thunder, Lightning, or in Raine?
2. When the Hurley-burley's done,
When the Battaile's lost, and wonne.
3. That will be ere the set of Sunne.
1. Where the place?
2. Vpon the Heath.
3. There to meet with *Macbeth*.
1. I come, *Gray-Malkin*.
All. Padock calls anon: faire is foule, and foule is faire,
Houer through the fogge and filthie ayre. *Exeunt.*

Scena Secunda.

*Alarum within. Enter King Malcolme, Donal-
baine, Lenox, with attendants, meeting
a bleeding Captaine.*

King. What bloody man is that? he can report,
As seemeth by his plight, of the Reuolt
The newest state.
Mal. This is the Serieant,
Who like a good and hardie Souldier fought
'Gainst my Captiuitie: Haile braue friend;
Say to the King, the knowledge of the Broyle,
As thou didst leaue it.
Cap. Doubtfull it stood,
As two spent Swimmers, that doe cling together,
And choake their Art: The mercilesse *Macdonwald*
(Worthie to be a Rebell, for to that
The multiplying Villanies of Nature
Doe swarme vpon him) from the Westerne Isles
Of Kernes and Gallowgrosses is supply'd,
And Fortune on his damned Quarry smiling,
Shew'd like a Rebells Whore: but all's too weake:
For braue *Macbeth* (well hee deserues that Name)
Disdayning Fortune, with his brandisht Steele,
Which smoak'd with bloody execution
(Like Valours Minion) caru'd out his passage,
Till hee fac'd the Slaue:
Which neu'r shooke hands, nor bad farwell to him,
Till he vnseam'd him from the Naue toth'Chops,
And fix'd his Head vpon our Battlements.

King. O valiant Cousin, worthy Gentleman.
Cap. As whence the Sunne 'gins his reflection,
Shipwracking Stormes, and direfull Thunders:
So from that Spring, whence comfort seem'd to come,
Discomfort swells: Marke King of Scotland, marke,
No sooner Iustice had, with Valour arm'd,
Compell'd these skipping Kernes to trust their heeles,
But the Norweyan Lord, surueying vantage,
With furbusht Armes, and new supplyes of men,
Began a fresh assault.
King. Dismay'd not this our Captaines, *Macbeth* and
Banquoh?
Cap. Yes, as Sparrowes, Eagles;
Or the Hare, the Lyon:
If I say sooth, I must report they were
As Cannons ouer-charg'd with double Cracks,
So they doubly redoubled stroakes vpon the Foe:
Except they meant to bathe in reeking Wounds,
Or memorize another *Golgotha*,
I cannot tell: but I am faint,
My Gashes cry for helpe.
King. So well thy words become thee, as thy wounds,
They smack of Honor both: Goe get him Surgeons.

Enter Rosse and Angus.

Who comes here?
Mal. The worthy *Thane* of Rosse.
Lenox. What a haste lookes through his eyes?
So should he looke, that seemes to speake things strange.
Rosse. God saue the King.
King. Whence cam'st thou, worthy *Thane?*
Rosse. From Fiffe, great King,
Where the Norweyan Banners flowt the Skie,
And fanne our people cold.
Norway himselfe, with terrible numbers,
Assisted by that most disloyall Traytor,
The *Thane* of Cawdor, began a dismall Conflict,
Till that *Bellona's* Bridegroome, lapt in proofe,
Confronted him with selfe-comparisons,
Point against Point, rebellious Arme 'gainst Arme,
Curbing his lauish spirit: and to conclude,
The Victorie fell on vs.
King. Great happinesse.
Rosse. That now *Sweno*, the Norwayes King,
Craues composition:
Nor would we deigne him buriall of his men,
Till he disbursed, at Saint *Colmes* ynch,
Ten thousand Dollars, to our generall vse.

King. No

A reproduction of the first page of *Macbeth* in the First Folio (1623).

Editing *Macbeth*

by David Scott Kastan

The earliest text of *Macbeth* is that which was published in the Folio of 1623, though the play was probably written sometime around 1606. It appears in the Folio as the seventh of the tragedies, printed between *Julius Caesar* and *Hamlet*. The Folio text derives from a playhouse script (or perhaps a transcript based on it) rather than from an authorial manuscript. The shortest of the tragedies (about 2,100 lines), *Macbeth* seems to reflect some theatrical cutting (especially in Act One) as well as to register some interpolations (3.5 and parts of 4.1, both of which contain songs by Thomas Middleton, which are printed in the appendix on pp. 287–290, and may include additional text by him or another playwright). No Quarto of *Macbeth* was printed prior to the Folio (it was registered in 1623 with The Stationers' Company among the sixteen plays "not formerly entred [*sic*] to other men"), so it is impossible to reconstruct the play as Shakespeare may have originally written it; but the Folio text is a reasonably clean version of the play as it was performed by Shakespeare's company in the early seventeenth century, probably similar to the version seen by Simon Forman, whose diary entry for April 20, 1611 (mistakenly recorded as 1610) provides the first known reference to a performance of *Macbeth*.

In general, the editorial work of this present edition is conservative, a matter of normalizing spelling, capitalization, and punctuation; removing superfluous italics; regularizing the names of characters, and rationalizing entrances and exits. A comparison of the edited text of 1.1.1.–1.2.62 with the facsimile page of the Folio (see page 294) reveals some of the issues in modernization. The speech prefixes are expanded for clarity, so that "1.", "2.", and "3." in the first scene become **First Witch**, **Second Witch**, and **Third Witch**; in the second scene "Mal." becomes **Malcolm**, and the Folio's "King" becomes **Duncan**. Spelling throughout is modernized. As spelling in Shakespeare's time had not yet been stabilized, words were spelled in various ways that indicated their proximate pronunciation, and compositors, in any case, were under no obligation to follow the spelling of their copy. Since the copy for *Macbeth* was a playhouse script (or a transcript of one), the spelling of the Folio text is probably at several removes from Shakespeare's own hand.

Little, then, is to be gained in an edition such as this by following the spelling of the original printed text. Therefore, "wonne" in line four of 1.1 unproblematically becomes "won"; "foule" in line 11, "foul"; "fogge" in line 12, "fog"; and "ayre," "air." Old spellings are consistently modernized, but old forms of words (i.e., "Norweyan" in 1.2.31) are retained. The capitalized first letters of many nouns in the Folio (e.g., "Thunder, Lightning, or in Raine") are reduced to lowercase, except where modern punctuation would demand them. The italics of proper names ("Macdonwald" in 1.2.9 or "Macbeth" in line 16) and of unusual words ("Thane" in line 45) are all removed. Punctuation, too, is adjusted to reflect modern practice (which is designed to clarify the logical relations between grammatical units, unlike seventeenth-century punctuation, which was dominated by rhythmical concerns), since the punctuation is no more likely than the spelling or capitalization to be Shakespeare's own. Thus, Malcolm's reply to Duncan at 1.2.3–7 reads in the Folio:

> This is the Serieant,
> Who like a good and hardie Souldier fought
> 'Gainst my Captiuitie : Haile braue friend ;
> Say to the King, the knowledge of the Broyle,
> As thou didst leaue it.

Modernized this reads:

> This is the sergeant
> Who like a good and hardy soldier fought
> 'Gainst my captivity. —Hail, brave friend!
> Say to the King the knowledge of the broil
> As thou didst leave it.

No doubt there is some loss in modernization. Clarity and consistency is gained at the expense of some loss of expressive detail, but normalizing spelling, capitalization, and punctuation allows the text to be read with far greater ease than the original, and essentially as it was intended to be understood. Seventeenth-century readers would have been unsurprised to find "u" for "v" in "Captiuitie" in line 5, nor been confused by the "ie" ending (also in "hardie" on line 4) where we would have a "y." "Serieant" in line 3 would be readily understood as "serjeant," "i" almost always being used where we would have a "j" (though the modern spelling of the word is, of course, "sergeant"). The intrusive "e"s in words like "Haile" (line 5) would not have seemed odd, nor would the "literary" capitalization of the noun. The colon and the semicolon in line 5 respectively mark a heavy and a slightly less heavy pause rather than define a precise (and different) grammatical relation as they do in modern usage. Modernizing in all these cases clarifies rather than alters Shakespeare's intentions. If inevitably in moderniza-tion we do lose the historical feel of the text Shakespeare's contempo-raries read, it is important to note that Shakespeare's contemporaries would not have thought the Folio in any sense archaic or quaint, as these details inevitably make it for a reader today. The text would have seemed to them as modern as this one does to us. Indeed, many of the Folio's typographical peculiarities are the result of its effort to make the printed page look up to date for potential buyers.

Modern readers, however, cannot help but be distracted by the different conventions they encounter on the Folio page. While it is indeed of interest to see how orthography and typography have changed over time, these changes are not primary concerns for most readers of this edition. What little, then, is lost in a careful modernization of the text is more than made up for by the removal of the artificial obstacle of unfamiliar spelling forms and punctuation habits, which Shakespeare never could have intended as interpretive difficulties for his readers.

Textual Notes

The list below records all substantive departures in this edition from the Folio text of 1623. It does not record modernizations of spelling, corrections of obvious typographical errors, adjustments of lineation, minor repositioning or rewording of stage directions, or rationalizations of speech prefixes. The adopted reading in this edition is given first in boldface and followed by the original, rejected reading of the Folio, or noted as being absent from the Folio text. Editorial stage directions are not collated but are enclosed within brackets in the text. Latin stage directions are translated (e.g., "They all exit" for *Exeunt omnes*), and the Latin act and scene designation of the Folio are similarly translated (e.g., Act One, scene one for *Actus primus, scena prima*).

1.1.9SP Second Witch All ; **1.1.10SP Third Witch** [not in F]; **1.1.11SP** All [in F at l.9]; **1.2.1SP (and throughout) Duncan** King; **1.2.13 gal-lowglasses** Gallowgrosses; **1.2.21 ne'er** neu'r; **1.2.26 thunders break** Thunders; **1.3.32 weird** weyward; **1.3.39 Forres** Soris;

1.3.98 Came Can; **1.3.111 lose** loose; **1.3.136 hair** Heire; **1.5.1SP** (and throughout); **Lady Macbeth** Lady; **1.5.8 weird** weyward; **1.5.11 lose** loose; **1.5.46 it** hit; **1.6.4 martlet** Barlet; **1.6.9 most** must; **1.7.6 shoal** Schoole; **1.7.22 cherubim** Cherubin; **1.7.47 do** no; **2.1.20 weird** weyward; **2.1.55 strides** sides; **2.1.56 sure** sowre; **2.1.57 way they** they may; **2.2.13SD** [in F at l.8]; **2.3.40SD** [in F at l. 39]; **2.3.139 nea'er** neere; **3.1.2 weird** weyard; **3.3.7 and** end; **3.4.78 time** times; **3.4.133 weird** weyard; **3.4.144 in deed** indeed; **3.6.24 son** Sonnes; **3.6.38 the** their; **4.1.93 Dunsinane** Dunsmane; **4.1.94SD descends** Descend; **4.1.98 (and throughout) Birnam** Byrnan (also spelled Byrnam, Birnan, Byrnan, and Birnane); **4.1.119 eighth** eight; **4.1.136 weird** Weyard; **4.2.1SP (and throughout) Lady Macduff** Wife; **4.2.82 shag-haired** shagge-ear'd; **4.3.4 downfall'n** downfall; **4.3.15 deserve** discerne; **4.3.34 affeered** affear'd; **4.3.34 Fare** Far; **4.3.133 thy** they; **4.3.160 not** nor; **4.3.168 rend** rent; **5.3.39 Cure her** Cure; **5.3.55 senna** Cyme; **5.4.16SP Siward** Sey.

Macbeth on the Early Stage
by Jesse M. Lander

obody knows when or where *Macbeth* was first performed. Some scholars have argued that the play was composed for presentation at the court of King James I during the visit of the King's brother-in-law, Christian IV of Denmark, in the summer of 1606, but there is no hard evidence to support such a performance. Contemporary allusions to the play appear to indicate that it was first performed before 1607, and allusions within the play to the Gunpowder Plot of November 1605 would place its composition in late 1605 or 1606. At the time, Shakespeare's acting company, the King's Men, were performing at the Globe, an open-air theater. Shortly afterward, in 1608, the company began to make arrangements for a second venue, the Blackfriars, an enclosed or "private" theater that relied on candlelight, and from 1609 on their plays were presumably written with some sense of the potentials and the pitfalls of both houses. The first solid evidence concerning performance comes in the form of a note written by Simon Forman, an astrologer and medical practitioner. Forman's memoranda were intended for "common policy," and he seems to have been chiefly interested in the practical wisdom afforded by the plays. Despite this nontheatrical purpose, the note indicates that the play was being staged

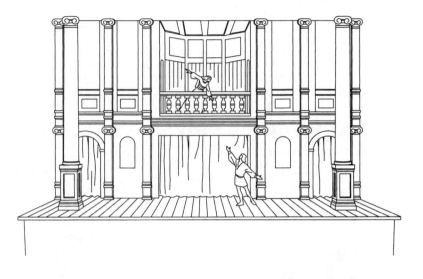

Fig 1. In the large London playhouses, the balcony above the stage could be used for staging, seating, or to house musicians.

Fig 2. English Renaissance drama made minimal use of sets or backdrops. In the absence of a set, the stage pillars could be incorporated into the action, standing in for trees and other architectural elements.

Fig 3. *The discovery space, located in the middle of the backstage wall, could be used as a third entrance as well as a location for scenes requiring special staging, such as in a tomb or bedchamber.*

Fig 4. *A trapdoor led to the area below the stage, known as "Hell" (as contrasted with the painted ceiling, known as "Heaven" or the "heavens"). Ghosts or other supernatural figures could descend through the trap, and it could also serve as a grave.*

at the Globe in April of 1611 and provides tantalizing clues about this early performance. Staging at the Globe in 1611 does not preclude performances at the Blackfriars, but taken in combination with the likelihood of an initial performance at the Globe in 1606, it does suggest that the play was emphatically, if not exclusively, a public theater production.

The Globe was an open-air amphitheater with an elevated thrust stage surrounded on three sides by spectators. Beneath the stage, an area known as "Hell" (see Fig 4) could be accessed through traps in the stage floor, allowing for descents. Above the stage, supported by two columns at the front, was a roof that protected the players from the weather and also served as the "heavens," and which was likely painted with a sun, moon, and stars. The back wall of the stage had doors for entrances and exits, providing access to the "tiring-house" or dressing room. An upper level of the stage façade had a balcony that could serve as a stage location but could also be used as seating for gentlemen (akin to a box seat in a modern theater) or as a space for musicians. Though the bareness of the Elizabethan stage has often been emphasized, curtains and wall hangings were used to decorate the stage façade, and these may have indicated specific places. However, the Tudor-Stuart theater did not strive for pictorial realism. Instead of sets, players used the space of the stage and a range of properties to suggest locale. The theater of the day was visually suggestive—it relied on the audience to respond to verbal cues, gestures, and props in order to imagine a setting. On an otherwise uncluttered stage, a particular piece of furniture, such as a bed or a throne, or a prop, such as a crown, a dagger, or a chalice, can assume the status of an emblem.

Macbeth does not require a large number of stage properties, yet four are particularly prominent and become extraordinary icons within the play: the daggers of Act Two, scene one and Act Two, scene two; the cup of Act Three, scene four; the cauldron in Act Four, scene one; and the boughs carried by the soldiers in Act Five, scene six. In each case, the object carries an extraordinary density of meaning. The dagger is not merely a weapon, a harbinger of violence; it is small, concealable, and its use requires an appalling intimacy. The cup is a symbol of conviviality and communion, but is susceptible to ironic inversion that transforms it into a "poisoned chalice" (1.7.11). The cauldron with its dreadful contents is the demonic antithesis of the feast that ratifies an integrated social order; a grossly enlarged version of the cup used for a false pledge, the cauldron gives concrete expression to "a deed without a name" (4.1.49). The boughs carried from Birnam Wood are vivid representations of an organic nature in which growth and flourishing unfold according to a steady order.

One of the most striking aspects of a performance of *Macbeth* at the Globe was that it took place in daylight. For stagecraft this is important because so much of the play's action occurs either at night or in the dark of a day turned into night. When Macbeth announces, "Light thickens, / And the crow makes wing to th' rooky wood" (3.2.50–51) he is inviting his audience to imagine the onset of darkness. The same technique is used when Ross observes, "By th' clock 'tis day, / And yet dark night strangles the traveling lamp" (2.4.6–7). The audience is asked to imagine a day that is unnaturally dark and murky. Darkness is also indicated by the presence of artificial light, such as the ubiquitous torches or Lady Macbeth's candle.

Though the effect of darkness draws upon the audience's willingness to accept theatrical convention, the play is not without special effects. The weird sisters are the most obvious element in the play that uses theatrical technology to create spectacle, especially in the sequence of apparitions in Act Four, scene one. The ghost of Banquo, though it does not appear to use the trap, also requires some special staging. Perhaps less immediately obvious but no less important are the enormous number of offstage sounds that punctuate the play. The very first of these appears in the initial stage direction: "Thunder and lightning." In the prologue to *Everyman in his Humor*, Ben Jonson mocks the various special effects that will not appear in his play:

Nor creaking throne comes down, the boys to please;
Nor nimble squib is seen, to make afear'd
The gentlewomen; nor roll'd bullet heard
To say, it thunders; nor tempestuous drum
Rumbles, to tell you when the storm doth come . . . .

Jonson points to two techniques used to simulate thunder: the rolling of a cannon ball and the beating of a drum. Several descriptions of the first technique exist, ranging from rolling a cannonball on the floor of an overhead chamber to the construction of an elaborate device in which a cannonball rolls through a series of drops. While the precise technique used for *Macbeth* remains uncertain, thunder is a prominent effect in the play and one that recurs throughout Shakespeare's work. Thunder, it should be pointed out, held a special menace for the early modern audience; according to George Gifford, a late sixteenth-century non-conformist Protestant, "It is a common opinion when there are mighty winds and thunders with terrible lightnings that the devil is abroad."

Thunder is the most prominent and ominous sound effect, but there are all sorts of other noises as well: bells, trumpets, drums, alarums, hautboys (a woodwind instrument of high pitch), the hoof beats of horses, and the knocking at the gate. When Macbeth asks Lady Macbeth whether she heard a noise, she replies, "I heard the owl scream and the crickets cry" (2.2.15), sounds that may have been supplied. Noises serve a variety of functions, but one repeated dynamic is a noise that interrupts the present action: a reminder that forces, sometimes unknown, are gathering offstage. The knocking at the gate immediately after Duncan's murder is the most famous example of this, and Macbeth says in response, "every noise appalls me" (2.2.61).

The cry of women in Act Five, scene five operates in a similar way. Macbeth asks, "What is that noise?" repeating his earlier question to Lady Macbeth, "Didst thou not hear a noise?" The unidentified noise in the dark points to a primordial fear of night's black agents, but Macbeth, who once felt an uncanny fear at the dismal sound of a "night-shriek," now declares himself hardened and implacable. The play's richly suggestive soundscape, contained in stage directions both explicit and implicit, easily escapes the attention of the reader, but it was an enormously important part of the early audience's experience of the play and remains central to modern performances.

As important as sound effects are, the play also provides lavish spectacle. The appearance of Banquo's ghost is a grim vision, a "horrible shadow." The ghost does not speak, and Macbeth's response focuses insistently on sight. The apparition apparently made an impression on the play's spectators. Simon Forman gives a vivid account of the scene: "The next night, being at supper with his noble men whom he had bid to a feast to which also Banco should have come, he began to speak of noble Banco, and to wish that he were there. And as he thus did, standing up to drink a carouse to him, the ghost of Banco came and sat down in his chair behind him. And he, turning about to sit down again, saw the ghost of Banco, which fronted him so that he fell into a passion of fear and fury." In Francis Beaumont's The *Knight of the Burning Pestle*, Jasper pretends to be a ghost in order to frighten his antagonist into repentance:

When thou art at thy table with thy friends,
Merry in heart, and filled with swelling wine,
I'll come in midst of all thy pride and mirth,
Invisible to all men but thy self,
And whisper such a sad tale in thine ear,
Shall make thee let the cup fall from thy hand,
And stand as mute and pale as death itself.

That Jasper enters with his face "mealed" may also provide a clue about the way in which the ghost of Banquo was staged. Though stage ghosts often appeared in shrouds, representing the winding cloth used in burial, Banquo would have worn the same clothes that he had on in Act Three, scene three. In addition to having his face whitened, the ghost presumably had bloody wounds and "gory locks," a gruesome spectacle rendered more horrifying by the ghost's refusal to speak and by the fact that the other dinner guests are unable to see it.

Though the ghost of Banquo clearly made an impression on early audiences, the weird sisters are the play's most prominent theatrical spectacle. In fact, textual evidence suggests that over the course of time the play was revised in order to expand the role of the witches and to make them more spectacular. Even if these later additions are discounted as nonauthorial accretions, the weird sisters from the start exploit stage technology to wonderful effect. They are accompanied by the ominous sound of thunder; their appearance, "withered" and "wild in their attire," causes puzzlement. Even their gender is confusing: Banquo says, "You should be women, / And yet your beards forbid me to interpret / That you are so" (1.3.45–47). If their appearance is cause for comment, their disappearance is downright mysterious. The stage direction "**Witches** vanish" (1.3.78) may indicate that they descend through a trapdoor. The startled reaction of Macbeth and Banquo indicates that their exit is sudden and inexplicable.

In addition to being themselves spectacular, the weird sisters stage a spectacle for Macbeth. The series of apparitions in Act Four, scene one made use of the trap in order to rise before Macbeth and then descend. The armed head, the bloody babe, and the crowned child holding a tree are conspicuously emblematic figures. The 18th-century critic John Upton declares, "The armed head represents symbolically Macbeth's head cut off and brought to Malcolm by Macduff. The bloody child is Macduff untimely ripped from his mother's womb. The child with the crown on his head, and a bough in his hand, is the royal Malcolm, who ordered his soldiers to hew them down a bough and bear it before them to Dunsinane." While these ascriptions are not incontestable, they do reveal an important logic. The severed head was a potent symbol of treason, and the decapitated heads of traitors were frequently affixed to poles on London Bridge. The first apparition provides a visual anticipation of the concluding moment in which Macduff presents Malcolm with the "usurper's cursèd head." However, like the prophecies themselves, these strange images only assume a clear significance in retrospect. In contrast, the meaning of the final series of apparitions, "A show of eight kings, and Banquo last; [the eighth king] with a glass in his hand," is made immediately clear: they are the royal offspring of Banquo. The "glass" is an enchanted mirror that shows Macbeth an endless succession of Stuart kings.

Apparently the witch business proved popular with audiences, and sometime after the initial staging of the play—probably after 1611, when Forman saw the play—Thomas Middleton, the dramatist who replaced Shakespeare as principal writer for the King's Men, appears to have added the Hecate scenes to the play. Three things about this interpolated material (3.5 and 4.1.39–43; 125–132) stand out. First, the total number of witches is multiplied; second, they sing and dance incessantly; third, Hecate flies. This last development may owe something to the installation of descent machinery at the Globe. Though the Rose Theatre had a throne for descents by 1595, the Globe appears not to have been equipped with descent machinery until 1608, a change that helps explain the prominence of flight in two of Shakespeare's late plays, *Cymbeline* and *The Tempest*.

Middleton's interpolations begin a process that was extended in the Restoration by William Davenant, who turned *Macbeth* into a quasi-opera. Davenant's version expanded the roles of the witches, took full advantage of new and sophisticated stage machinery, and transformed the moral complexity of Shakespeare's play into melodrama. Macbeth, for example, dies proclaiming, "Farewell vain world, and what's most vain in it: ambition." Though this newly operatic *Macbeth* provoked the derision of some, Restoration audiences were thrilled. Samuel Pepys, the diarist, attended the play repeatedly; on one occasion he remarks, "Saw *Macbeth*, which though I saw it lately, yet appears a most excellent play in all respects, but especially in divertissement, though it be a deep tragedy." Later in the same year, he writes, "Here we saw *Macbeth*, which though I have seen it often, yet it is one of the best plays for a stage, and variety of dancing and music, that ever I saw." As the seventeenth century draws to a close, Shakespeare's "secret, black, and midnight hags" (4.1.48) are turned into a crowd-pleasing extravaganza, and it can be no surprise that in the eighteenth century the witches were increasingly considered ridiculous.

Significant Performances
by Jesse M. Lander

1611   Globe Theatre, the King's Men—Richard Burbage, the leading man of Shakespeare's company, presumably played the role of Macbeth in this performance attended by Simon Forman. Forman was a doctor whose extensive diaries provide one of the few contemporary accounts of original Shakespearean performances.

1664   Lincoln Inn's Fields, Duke of York's Servants—William Davenant's revival of a revised *Macbeth*. In addition to expanding the witch scenes, Davenant wrote new material for Lady Macduff, providing a fuller representation of female virtue. Davenant also made adjustments throughout the text in order to clarify the moral of the play. This version was enormously popular, and Davenant's revision continued to be staged for the next eighty years.

1744   Drury Lane—David Garrick, the most famous English actor of the eighteenth century, staged a *Macbeth* that was described in playbills "as written by Shakespeare." While Garrick reduced the role of the singing and dancing witches and cut the Lady Macduff additions made by Davenant, he made his own alterations and additions. In particular, he gave the dying Macbeth a fulsome and pious confession of guilt. Garrick was widely praised for the realism of his portrayal of a noble and sensitive Macbeth under the sway of a terrifying Lady Macbeth played by Hannah Pritchard. Garrick's Macbeth soon came to be regarded as the benchmark for subsequent performances.

1773   Covent Garden—Charles Macklin, an Irish actor and playwright, produced a *Macbeth* that broke with the tradition of staging the play in modern dress. Macklin's Macbeth appeared in "the old Caledonian habit," wearing tartan stockings and a Scotch bonnet. Though this production was not a success, Macklin's interest in a historically "authentic" Macbeth was an important innovation, and subsequent productions followed Macklin's lead by adopting distinctively Scottish costumes.

1785   London—Sarah Siddons, an eighteenth-century star whose success on the stage made her into a cultural icon, continued the tradition of powerful Lady Macbeths begun by Hannah Pritchard. Siddons's charisma in the role eclipsed the Macbeth played by her brother John Philip Kemble. Siddons is remembered for having reworked the stage business of the sleepwalking scene. As played by Pritchard, Lady Macbeth carried her taper throughout; Siddons instead put the taper down to allow for vigorous hand-washing gestures. Her Lady Macbeth, full of passionate intensity, was a dominating presence.

1794   Drury Lane—John Philip Kemble's production did not stage Banquo's ghost, but in subsequent years the ghost was restored. Kemble's experiment with an invisible ghost was controversial at the time, but versions of *Macbeth* without the ghost became increasingly common in the nineteenth and twentieth centuries.

1843   Theatre Royal, Edinburgh—Helen Faucit introduced a new, feminine Lady Macbeth who subordinated her own natural inclinations in order to support her husband. Faucit's Lady Macbeth was a radical departure from the Pritchard-Siddons tradition that portrayed her as a domineering matriarch.

1849   Astor Place Theatre, New York—William Charles Macready, an English actor and theater manager, toured America in 1848–49. A quarrel with the American actor Edwin Forrest led to competing performances of *Macbeth* in Philadelphia, but matters came to a head when Macready played Macbeth in New York's Astor Place Theatre; showered with debris by hostile members of the audience, Macready was forced to end the performance. At the very same time, Forrest was playing Macbeth at the Broadway Theatre. Three days later, Macready again took the stage as Macbeth; increased security had reduced the number of troublemakers in the audience, but a mob soon gathered outside and began pelting the theater with cobblestones. Macready completed his performance, but a failed attempt at crowd control led to a riot in which more than thirty people were killed.

1888   Lyceum Theatre—Sir Henry Irving played Macbeth opposite Ellen Terry in a controversial production that explicitly rejected the "fiendlike queen" interpretation of Lady Macbeth. While Terry's Lady was gentle and feminine, Irving's Macbeth was conscience stricken and frequently criticized for appearing cowardly. Irving's portrayal of the witches departed from the usual spectacle in order to emphasize their demonic mystery. In an American staging of the show, Irving used a green light on a stool for Banquo's ghost.

1911   Her Majesty's Theatre—Herbert Beerbohm Tree, an actor and theater manager, produced a *Macbeth* that was widely recognized for its spectacular and realistic scenery. Beerbohm Tree's attention to the visual possibilities afforded by Shakespearean drama was accompanied by an interest in the new medium of film. In 1914, with D. W. Griffith, he filmed a version of *Macbeth* unrelated to the 1911 production, and some brief clips of his 1899 revival of *King John* are notable for being the earliest example of Shakespeare on film.

1933   Shakespeare   Memorial   Theatre,   Stratford—Theodore Komisarjevsky, a theater producer and designer, presented a provocative *Macbeth* on a bare stage dominated by surrealistic aluminum shapes. The all-aluminum set was sparsely lit, and the silver-gray costumes gave the production a uniform palette. Though the production was treated harshly by critics committed to picturesque realism, Komisarjevsky's work has since been recognized as an important innovation that anticipated significant trends in the modern theater.

1936   Lafayette Theatre, New York—Orson Welles directed an all-black cast in what has come to be known as the "voodoo" *Macbeth*. The action was transposed to nineteenth-century Haiti, and the witches were portrayed as voodoo priestesses under the direction of a male Hecate. Welles also increased their involvement in the play's action, and the incessant sounds of drums and chanting were used to create an atmosphere at once exotic and terrifying.

1955   Shakespeare   Memorial   Theatre,   Stratford—Glen Byam Shaw directed Laurence Olivier and Vivien Leigh in a hugely successful *Macbeth*. By casting two famous stars in the lead roles, Shaw sought to gain the audience's sympathy and admiration for Macbeth and Lady Macbeth. Olivier played Macbeth as hesitant at first, but progressively gaining in energy and intensity right up until the final battle. At the same time, the production emphasized the way in which as he rises, Lady Macbeth falls. For instance, Shaw had Leigh sink to her knees at the close of Act Three, scene four just before Olivier, having recovered from the appearance of Banquo's ghost, summons her to bed—an emblematic bit of stage business not demanded by the text.

1971   Roman Polanski, *Macbeth*—The most famous film version of the play. The thanes of Scotland engage in an endless and graphically violent contest for power in a damp and dirty Scotland. The character of Ross is transformed into a murderous opportunist who does Macbeth's dirty work before abandoning his master for Malcolm. The predictions are depicted as psychedelic hallucinations inspired by drinking the witches' brew, and the witches themselves are naturalized, a point emphasized by their nakedness when Macbeth sees them the second time. The final sequence famously shows a limping Donalbain seeking out the witches.

1976   The Other Place, Stratford-upon-Avon—Trevor Nunn directed Ian McKellen and Judi Dench in a minimalist staging that focused on the emotional intensity of the actors. The Other Place—the smallest of the Royal Shakespeare Company's three theaters—was equipped with a small square stage with seating for only 180 in the round. A black circle on the white stage delimited the playing area, and "offstage" actors stood or sat around the perimeter. While the production rejected lavish effects, it succeeded in making the witches truly terrifying and intrinsic to the play.

1999   Swan Theatre, Stratford-upon-Avon—Gregory Doran directed Antony Sher and Harriet Walters in a modern dress *Macbeth* set in a militaristic Balkan country and performed in the Royal Shakespeare Company's mid-sized performance space. Sher played Macbeth as a soldier turned dictator, a mentally unstable man of brutal ambition and black humor. The decision to dispense with an intermission increased the momentum of this fast-paced production.

Inspired by *Macbeth*

Stage

The widely held superstition that *Macbeth* bears a mysterious curse represents one of the strangest legacies of Shakespeare's play. It has become taboo among actors to speak the name *Macbeth* or to quote from the play inside a theater, except while performing it. Anyone who breaks this rule must leave the building, spin around three times, and spit or swear. According to legend, the curse against *Macbeth* began during one of its earliest runs, when a young boy died while playing the role of Lady Macbeth. Lack of evidence to support the story has not prevented it from enduring, and the supposed curse has been blamed for a litany of disasters in the years since. The most dramatic episode attributed to the curse—known as the Astor Place riots—occurred in 1849 at a New York performance of *Macbeth* starring William Charles Macready, the famous English tragedian. As the play got underway at the Astor Place Theatre, supporters of Edwin Forrest, a popular American actor involved in a heated rivalry with Macready, took to the streets and began throwing stones at the theater's walls. As their protest degenerated into a nationalist, anti-British frenzy, the crowd grew to an estimated 20,000. The National Guard arrived to control the violence and the ensuing riot, which left thirty-one dead and 150 injured. The curse has not spared modern productions, and most famously traumatized a 1937 performance at London's Old Vic, starring Laurence Olivier. A series of setbacks—including a close call in which the star himself was nearly crushed by a stage weight—culminated in the death of Lillian Baylis, the founder of the Old Vic, just before opening night.

Perhaps in reaction to the doom and melodrama of both the play and its performance history, twentieth-century playwrights have sometimes subverted the severity and spectacle of *Macbeth* by recasting the story as comedy, albeit a dark one. Barbara Garson's 1966 antiestablishment drama *MacBird* mocks the presidency of Lyndon Johnson, beginning with his bid for the 1960 Democratic nomination. When MacBird loses the race for king to the young upstart John Ken O'Dunc, Macbird's wife launches a plan to assassinate the victor so that her husband can usurp the throne. Once he takes power, however, MacBird's reign suffers from the uproar surrounding the war in Vietland and ruins his grand plans for a "Smooth Society" (an allusion to Johnson's 1964 "Great Society" speech). Lady MacBird's increasing neuroses cause her to do such things as obsessively spray air freshener throughout the royal quarters in an attempt to eradicate that "damned odor." Meanwhile, Bobby Ken O'Dunc secretly conspires on the sidelines to thwart MacBird. Controversial when it was first published, *MacBird* ran as both an off-Broadway and Broadway production, winning an Obie Award and a Tony nomination. Because of its political subject matter, the literary quality of the play is sometimes overlooked, along with Garson's admirable accomplishment in writing the entire drama in Elizabethan blank verse.

Conceived in the spirit of the Theater of the Absurd, a drama movement of the 50s and 60s that emphasized the meaningless randomness of life, Eugene Ionesco's *Macbett* (1972) embellishes *Macbeth* with dark, surrealist humor. Ionesco wreaks havoc on the details of *Macbeth* while preserving its themes and overall structure. For example, Ionesco's Lady Macbett is initially married to King Duncan but conspires with Banco and Macbett to murder her husband, after which she becomes the wife of Macbett. Ionesco complicates the plot further with flourishes of the ridiculous, such as the reduplication of every scene involving Macbett and Banco (simply because, in Ionesco's adaptation, they are twins). But the presence of absurdity does not preclude tragedy in *Macbett*. Minutes into the opening act, characters begin shouting at one another, assaulting the audience as well as each other. The verbal violence of the play is compounded by gratuitous scenes of blood and gore, as well as the generally savage nature of the main characters. Flashes of idealism and altruistic impulses are met with scorn, and the conclusion of the play does not offer even the traditional comforts of classical tragedy, where battle and bloodshed at least result in order being restored. In Shakespeare's *Macbeth*, the murder of the lawful King Duncan is righted by the restoration of the King's son to the throne. Ionesco's *Macbett*, however, concludes with a speech by the new King, the even more corrupt Macol, who professes that in all likelihood he, too, will be a terrible tyrant as the crowd serenades him with chants of "Long live Macol!"

Another darkly comedic adaptation of *Macbeth* is Tom Stoppard's *Cahoot's Macbeth* (1979), usually performed in concert with his *Hamlet* take off, *Dogg's Hamlet* (1979). Stoppard's play is a tribute to Paul Kohout, a Czechoslovakian playwright who was persecuted after the 1969 Soviet invasion imposed heavy restrictions on intellectual and artistic activities in that country. In response to the creative oppression of the Communist police state, actors and intellectuals would secretly stage mini-productions of plays in their own houses. *Cahoot's Macbeth* takes place during a clandestine performance of *Macbeth*. The play opens on a disheveled rendering of the first scene of *Macbeth*, staged in a cramped living room. Only when an inspector barges on the scene, interrupting the action and interrogating the actors, does it become clear that this *Macbeth* is actually a "play within a play." In order to circumvent the inspector's investigation, the players learn (thanks to a visit by a character from *Dogg's Hamlet*, performed in the first half) to speak Dogg, a gibberish language that the inspector cannot understand and therefore cannot censor. Liberated by this simulation of free speech, the actors continue with their performance of *Macbeth* unimpeded.

Richard Nathan's *Scots on the Rocks* (2000) is a full-length parody of *Macbeth* in the style of Abbott and Costello. The five-act charade maintains the play's basic storyline and even preserves some of Shakespeare's original dialogue, but creates comedy by exaggerating the action, interpreting poetic language literally, and injecting anachronistic references. For example, Nathan's Weird Sisters are rock and roll witches, constantly singing and dancing to what the stage directions call "a boogie-woogie beat." Among their acts of mischief is the literal unsexing of Lady Macbeth, when they cast a spell that turns her into a man. Wordplay and slapstick overwhelm the more dramatic elements, often developing into outright farce. The following exchange, immediately after Duncan's murder, is typical of the play's style:

> **Macbeth:** I can't go back there. There's blood everywhere. There's blood on the King's sheets, and his shirt, and that little skirt he wears. . . .
> **Lady Macbeth:** His kilt.
> **Macbeth:** I know he's kilt! I'm the guy that kilt him!

The scene quickly degenerates into physical scuffle, with the Macbeths smearing blood all over one another.

Film

One of the most acclaimed adaptations of *Macbeth* is Akira Kurosawa's 1957 film *Throne of Blood*, set in medieval Japan during a period of civil wars and aristocratic infighting. Kurosawa includes almost none of Shakespeare's language and alters several key elements of the plot. The weird sisters become a single Forest Spirit, a hag at a spinning wheel who vanishes immediately after issuing her prophecy. Washizu

(Macbeth) and Miki (Banquo) gallop after her wildly in an extended sequence of rushing forest landscape and obscuring fog and rain, which proves as disorienting for the viewer as the riders. The climax of Kurosawa's film differs substantially from that of Shakespeare's play as well. Instead of dying in single combat, Washizu is killed in a torrent of arrows shot by his own samurai. In spite of drastic alterations to the original play, *Throne of Blood* faithfully conveys the atmosphere and rhythm of *Macbeth*, using visual techniques drawn from the traditional Noh drama.

Developed in Japan in the fourteenth century, Noh plays depict stories drawn from history and myth and use visual symbolism rather than narrative and dialogue. All performances are governed by rigid rules covering everything from hand gestures to stage makeup. In *Throne of Blood*, the characters' facial makeup imitates specific Noh masks, and their costumes and posture reflect Noh conventions. *Throne of Blood* incorporates musical elements of Noh as well. Instead of using a lengthy monologue, Lady Macbeth's emotions are illustrated with a duet between the *nohkan* (ritual flute) and two types of Noh drums. Kurosawa transposes Shakespeare's story onto the Noh subgenre of *shura-mono*, in which the ghosts of famous warriors enact memories of violence as part of their quest for redemption. *Throne of Blood* draws on additional Noh subcategories, including those dealing with desperate women, madness, and demonic possession, to treat other themes from *Macbeth*.

Two Western films recast the *Macbeth* story as a gangster movie. Ken Hughes's *Joe Macbeth* (1955) and William Reilly's *Men of Respect* (1990) both make the Macbeth character a hitman, who attempts, with his wife's help, to climb the ranks of mob hierarchy. *Joe Macbeth* is set in Chicago in the 1930s. Joe's wife incites him to kill the Duncan character (Joe's boss, "the Duke") during a swim, and when Joe leaves the knife behind, she dives in to retrieve it. Joe grows paranoid as he becomes more powerful and murders the Banquo character, his best friend "Banky," whose ghost reappears at a dinner party that same night. Joe's wife mirrors Lady Macbeth's descent into madness, suffering from nightmares in which her hands are covered with blood. Both she and Joe are finally killed during a shoot-out with rival gangsters. Supernatural forces play a marginal role in *Joe Macbeth*, with the witches rendered as street vendors, and Hecate as a sandwich board man. The movie's one significant departure from Shakespeare's story is its conclusion, in which Banky's son refuses to accept job of crimeboss and walks away from the gangster life.

Men of Respect imitates *Joe Macbeth* in the careful way its plot corresponds with Shakespeare's play, but the latter movie glamorizes the story a bit more. Mike and his wife, Ruthie, are likeably ambitious, and instead of encountering three witches, Mike has visions after falling in with the members of a debauched cult. The visions tell him he will be invincible until the stars fall from heaven. (He is later killed during a firework display). Unlike *Joe Macbeth*, *Men of Respect* closely imitates Shakespeare's language, translating the verse of *Macbeth* into street slang while incorporating certain words and phrases from Shakespeare's original text. The end of Reilly's film directly opposes Hughes's, with "Mal," the Malcolm character, becoming the head of the local mob after "Duffie," the Macduff character, kills Macbeth in a climactic gun fight.

Music

Beethoven took inspiration from *Macbeth* for his 1808 Piano Trio in D Major (Opus 70, Number 1) also known as "The Ghost." The nickname refers to the eerie middle section of the work, which some have called the slowest movement in all of Beethoven. Gothic and brooding, the themes for this central D-minor movement were probably lifted from sketches Beethoven made for a *Macbeth* opera. "The Ghost" evokes the general mood of darkness and mystery that underlines Shakespeare's play, the weird sisters in particular. Like the *Macbeth*-inspired pieces by Bedrich Smetana and Richard Strauss (see below), Beethoven's trio is complex and innovative, but unlike their works his was met with critical acclaim and is frequently performed by major chamber music groups today.

By far the most important musical adaptation is Giuseppe Verdi's *Macbeth* opera. The 1847 composition was the first of three Verdi operas based on Shakespeare (*Othello* and *Falstaff* followed). Verdi infamously declared that the voice of Lady Macbeth should be low, hollow, and gravelly, with a devilish quality, but only after he overcame his initial feeling that she should not sing at all. In spite of this prejudice he ended up including a rich atmospheric aria for her in the second act, as well as a notable duet with Macbeth. Lady Macbeth's role constitutes one of the opera's most exciting elements. Verdi also makes Hecate and her witches major characters in his adaptation, furthering the opera's melodramatic spectacle. Less successful is Verdi's attempt to recast the tragedy of Macbeth as the triumph of Macduff. The opera's cheerful climax seeks to reassert the conquest of good over evil rather than developing the themes of betrayal, guilt, and madness that are so important to Shakespeare's *Macbeth*.

Bedrich Smetana used *Macbeth* as a platform for an experimental musical composition. His 1859 *Macbeth and the Witches: A Sketch from Shakespeare*, for piano and orchestra, reflected his desperation over the recent death of his wife. Smetana limits the scope of his work, focusing on the role of the supernatural in the play rather than on attempting to convey specific elements of the plot. Smetana's interpretation of the relationship between Macbeth and the weird sisters is impressionistic and atonal, making the piece difficult to perform and difficult for the listener to understand.

One of the more innovative musical adaptations is Richard Strauss's 1890 *Macbeth* tone poem (an orchestral composition that conveys nonmusical ideas through music). Some critics consider the piece Strauss's modernist manifesto, in which he asserts the importance of the dramatic qualities of a musical composition over its adherence to classical forms. It is nevertheless difficult to match up the structural elements of Strauss's *Macbeth* with the plot of Shakespeare's play, which is perhaps one of the reasons why the tone poem is so rarely performed. However, some moments are clearly marked. Macbeth's coronation, for example, is a stately 3/4 march in B flat, and the musical motifs from this section are later recapitulated and expanded during Macbeth's descent into madness. The tone poem opens and closes with expansive and meditative sections reminiscent of Wagner and Beethoven, which is appropriate, given those composers' interests in the effects of ambition and abuses of power.

For Further Reading
by Jesse M. Lander

Adelman, Janet. "'Born of Woman': Fantasies of Maternal Power in *Macbeth*." *Cannibals, Witches, and Divorce: Estranging the Renaissance*. Ed. Marjorie Garber. Baltimore: Johns Hopkins University Press, 1987. 90–121. A psychoanalytic reading that examines the play's attempt to construct an autonomous male identity against the threat of maternal power, as embodied by the witches and Lady Macbeth.

Booth, Stephen. *"King Lear," "Macbeth", Indefinition, and Tragedy*. New Haven: Yale University Press, 1983. For Booth, tragedy is "an experience of the fact of indefinition," and his careful reading of *Macbeth* reveals an inconclusive play that frustrates our desire for clarity and understanding.

Bradley, A. C. *Shakespearean Tragedy*. London: MacMillan and Co., 1904. A classic piece of Shakespearean criticism focused on questions of character; Bradley's Macbeth is a figure of tragic grandeur endowed with a poetic imagination, and his Lady Macbeth is both appalling and sublime.

Brooks, Cleanth. "The Naked Babe and the Cloak of Manliness." *The Well Wrought Urn*. Ed. Cleanth Brooks. New York: Reynal & Hitchcock, 1947. 21–46. A famous essay arguing that the play ought to be read as a poem in which metaphor and symbol are central to the text's structure and meaning.

Gardner, Helen. "Milton's 'Satan' and the Theme of Damnation in Elizabethan Tragedy." *English Studies* New Series 1 (1948): 46–99. Examines Macbeth as one of several examples of the Elizabethan fascination with those who knowingly act against nature and are incapable of repentance.

Greenblatt, Stephen. "Shakespeare Bewitched." *New Historical Literary Study*. Eds. Jeffrey N. Cox and Larry J. Reynolds. Princeton: Princeton University Press, 1993. Argues that Shakespeare, as a dramatist who trades in illusion and spectacle, bears an uncanny resemblance to the witches themselves.

Hawkins, Michael. "History, Politics, and *Macbeth*." *Focus on "Macbeth."* Ed. John Russell Brown. London: Routledge & Kegan Paul, 1982. 155–88. Places *Macbeth* within the context of both social history and the history of political thought; concludes that the royalism often imputed to the play has been exaggerated.

Knights, L. C. *How Many Children Had Lady Macbeth? An Essay in the Theory and Practice of Shakespeare Criticism*. Cambridge: The Minority Press, 1933. Criticizes the character-based criticism exemplified by Bradley and argues for an approach more attentive to the language of the play; as a dramatic poem, *Macbeth* is "a statement not of philosophy but of ordered emotion."

McCoy, Richard C. "'The Grace of Grace' and Double-Talk in *Macbeth*." *Shakespeare Survey* 57 (2004): 27–37. Argues that Malcolm, an actor and player-king, is the true hero of the play; Malcolm's concluding invocation of the "grace of Grace" is an equivocation, but it points to the restorative potential of words gracefully performed.

Norbrook, David. "*Macbeth* and the Politics of Historiography." *Politics of Discourse: The Literature and History of Seventeenth-Century England*. Ed. Kevin Sharpe and Steven Zwicker. Berkeley: University of California Press, 1987. 78–116. Argues that the political attitudes embedded in the sources available to Shakespeare are less assuredly monarchical than has been previously recognized.

Orgel, Stephen. "*Macbeth* and the Antic Round." *Shakespeare Survey* 52 (1999): 143–54. Stresses the play's failure to celebrate James I's lineage and questions the common notion that the play ends with the clear triumph of good over evil.

Sinfield, Alan. "*Macbeth*: History, Ideology and Intellectuals." *Critical Quarterly* 28 (1986): 63–77. Examines the ways in which *Macbeth* exposes the contradictions inherent in violence sanctioned by the state; argues that both conservative and liberal critics of the play have been complicit with state ideologies.

Stallybrass, Peter. "*Macbeth* and Witchcraft." *Focus on "Macbeth."* Ed. John Russel Brown. London: Routledge & Kegan Paul, 1982. 189–209. Argues that witchcraft in *Macbeth* legitimates patriarchy and serves as a form of ideological closure.

Waith, Eugene M. "Manhood and Valor in Two Shakespearean Tragedies." *English Literary History* 17 (1950): 262–73. Argues that the play presents competing accounts of manhood: a narrowly militaristic ideal embodied by Macbeth and a comprehensive ideal embodied by Macduff, whose physical courage is matched by a sympathy for others and a sense of moral obligation.

Wills, Gary. *Witches and Jesuits: Shakespeare's "Macbeth."* Oxford: Oxford University Press, 1995. Identifies *Macbeth* as one of a series of plays written in response to the Gunpowder Plot and explores the play's theological politics.